Stealth Coaching

Everyday Conversations for Extraordinary Results

By Rob Kramer

First published by Dog Ear Publishing
4010 W. 86th Street, Ste H
Indianapolis, IN 46268
www.dogearpublishing.net

ISBN: 978-1-4575-1637-5

This book is printed on acid-free paper.

Printed in the United States of America

Table of Contents

Acknowledgements

Introduction

i.   Foreword by Ron Redmon viii

ii. Preface: What Would Make This Book Worth Your While?...x

iii. If You Only Read the First Page of this Book, Here are Ten Things to Remember xiii

Section I: What It Is and Why Do It

1. The Win-Win Power of Coaching...........................2

2. Why Coaching? 6

3. What is Coaching? 9

4. What is Stealth Coaching? 15

5. How Does Stealth Coaching Differ From Other Forms of Coaching? 19

6. What Are Noticeable Results of Stealth Coaching?..............23

7. Coaching vs. Mentoring......................................27

8. The Business Case to be a Coaching Leader 30

Section II: How It Works

9. The Coaching Mindset: How Mentality Influences Choices, Actions, and Outcomes...........................36

10. Mindfulness Affects Attention and Focus 40

11. Conscious Listening...46

12. Driving the Coaching Conversation to Action:
    The Art and Science of Inquiry 53

Section III: Implementation

13. First Steps: The Assessment of Readiness............................66

14. Introducing and Unveiling Stealth Coaching
    in the Workplace...69

15. When to Stealth Coach 73

16. Who to Stealth Coach First......................................78

17. Stealth Coaching With Peers...................................80

18. Stealth Coaching With Superiors 82

Section IV: Barriers and Challenges

19. The Leader's Dilemma: Challenges in the Information
    and Multitasking Age..90

20. Overcoming Predictable Barriers and Challenges.................92

21. Yeah, But 97

22. A Note on Patience 107

Closing

• Afterward: A Note from the Author..............................110

• References..111

• About the Author 115

ACKNOWLEDGEMENTS

This book has been a labor of love and commitment, and one that has come to be with a tremendous amount of help.

Thank you to those who have provided irreplaceable input, advice, and feedback, including: Kim Strom-Gottfried, Abigail T. Panter, Patrick Louden, William Frey, Chris Melissinos, Karen Tax, and Phil Evans.

Thank you to Barbara A. Zelter: for not only being my editor, but in many ways my literary escort and co-author.

To Warren Blank and Aaron Brown: I am humbled by your guidance, camaraderie, leadership and brotherhood – beyond my wildest dreams. A million thanks.

To Ron Redmon: may this book provide one small example of the impact you have had on my work and the person I am becoming. I continue to show up and see what emerges.

To my family: thank you for your investment of love, support, and patience. I could not have done it without you.

Lastly, to my beloved, Robin: words are never enough. There is a field…

INTRODUCTION

Foreword

It is a delight to contribute a few words for the front of this fresh entry in the literature of coaching. Rob and I met in 2004 and shortly thereafter he joined me in co-teaching a course in coaching that I had initiated at the Federal Executive Institute several years earlier.

Over the next four years, we introduced the concepts, techniques, and skills of coaching to hundreds of public sector senior managers and leaders. In the process, we learned more and more about the art and science of this discipline of empowerment and the possibilities that lie within it.

We approached each of our collaborations as an opportunity to present the material in a different way – to add, amend, or remove content based on what each of us had learned since our previous engagement, or to model different coaching behaviors. Expanding, deepening, and enriching our understanding of the field with what we took from the classroom was the ultimate compensation for our partnership, and I am proud of Rob for putting his storehouse of knowledge and experience into words so that others might now benefit.

Whenever we taught, Rob and I brought a number of books on coaching from our personal collections so that course participants could look through them at their leisure. We wanted them to see some of the best available resources in the field and also to be exposed to a variety of approaches. Among the frustrations we had with many of these books was that they made arcane reading for practicing managers, or were long on theory and short on application. Further, most of them offered one or more models or formulas as a kind of

"Rosetta stone" for the learner. Few of them translated and distilled the principles of human psychology into actionable lessons grounded in instructive stories, described the core skills of coaching so they are accessible to all, or provided tips for immediate action.

Rob has now written the book we wished for.

Ron Redmon
August 24, 2012
Flat Rock, North Carolina

Preface:
What Would Make This Book Worth Your While?

In my experience, both as a manager for fifteen years, and as an executive coach, I see more improvements and sustained change from coaching than from any other tool for leadership effectiveness. When I first discovered coaching for the workplace, I thought it was going to be another one of those flavor-of-the-month training schemes or improvement quick-fix programs. It was the 1990's. I saw coaching, with its limited resources available in the marketplace, as fitting into this same tired mold: everyone gets trained and tries it at work for a period of time; management will "check the box" that the workforce has been exposed to coaching; and then on to the next great leadership development solution.

However, coaching has stuck around. As of August 2012, typing "coaching" into the search engine at Amazon.com results in more than 19,000 available resources. So why has there been such growth and sustainability in this seemingly niche field? Perhaps because studies on the use of coaching as a professional development tool show that when on-the-job experience, mentoring, or training is supported by coaching, the retention levels of newly learned skills and experiences are near 90%.[1] Coaching has also shown organizational return on investments exceeding 120% for every dollar spent.[2]

After learning these statistics, as well as experiencing coaching myself, I realized: How can I ignore this stuff any longer? It works. And it works really, really well.

Still, I found through lots and lots of failures that I could not always be transparent when utilizing coaching skills. People would look at me like I had two heads, or at times I flirted with being known as "the guy who doesn't give answers, he only asks questions." That is not a useful reputation to have, especially when working in management. I had to develop a methodology and framework to use coaching without others necessarily knowing I was coaching. Thus, fifteen years, hundreds of formal coaching clients, and thousands of informal workplace coaching conversations later (some with better results than others!), the concept for *Stealth Coaching* has emerged:

> *Stealth Coaching is an **informal, everyday conversation process** that can be utilized in almost any context where the coachee has a situation in which more than one solution is possible.*

This book is designed as a useful tool for anyone wanting to make positive changes in the world, or simply in the day to day grind of work. As a busy professional myself, I have found it hard to return to the usual coaching, management and leadership books on my shelves, as they are usually: (1) long, (2) theoretical, and (3) hard to efficiently glean for takeaways. My goal with this book is to make it pragmatic, valuable, convenient, and something the reader wants to keep close at hand.

To make it applicable to any reader, the context is written for the "leader," that being anyone who has (or has the potential to) gain willing followers towards the accomplishment of a goal or mission. If helpful, you may consider substituting the word "manager" or "coach" whenever you read the word leader.

To be clear, though, the role of leader, manager, and coach are mutually exclusive of one another. For example, consider bad managers who thought they were great leaders. Recall front-line employees who actually *were* great leaders, stepping up and gaining followers from across the organization. Anyone can be a leader because anyone can gain willing followers. Additionally, anyone, regardless of role, has the ability to be an effective coach. Thus, anyone can derive value from this book: executive, employee, manager, peer, partner, and so on.

Stealth Coaching is divided into sections, to separate components so the reader can easily locate topics of interest.

Section one establishes the framework of stealth coaching, answering key questions of "what is it" and "why bother using it."

Section two addresses how coaching stealthfully works, clarifying its foundational components.

Section three's focus is on application: when to use it, strategies for starting out, and using it with different audiences.

Section four tackles barriers to effective stealth coaching, such as overcoming challenges and addressing common resistors or "yeah, but" excuses. In my experience teaching coaching classes and workshops to executives, senior managers, front line supervisors, staff and students, these are typical questions, challenges, and resistors that I have heard as people investigate the value of stealth coaching.

Each chapter concludes with "Dog Ear These Ideas:" a set of practical applications to put into practice.

I hope you find this book to be a useful reference in your growth as a leader, manager, coach, colleague, or friend. I appreciate your questions, insight, feedback, and stories. Please feel free to email me at StealthCoachingBook@gmail.com.

If You Only Read the First Page of this Book, Here are Ten Things to Remember

10. The typical employee's knowledge transfer goes from 25% through training alone to 90% with the support of coaching. Leaders cannot afford *not* to add this tool to their toolbox.

9. Jump to the chapter, "Yeah, But…" for solutions to common barriers and objections people often have to becoming a coaching leader.

8. Coaching is not mentoring. A mentor provides advice. A coach helps the coachee to think and advise him or herself. This relieves the coach from having to have all the answers and allows the coachee to grow and develop his or her own capacities.

7. To empathize, to stand in someone else's shoes, the coach has to be willing to take off his or her own shoes first.

6. A simple strategy to make coaching a habit is to always start any interaction by asking at least one question.

5. It is hard to be an effective coach when one comes from the ideology that providing answers is more important than inviting reflection.

4. It is much easier to coach, to give feedback, to influence, or to ask favors of others if there is at least a basic level of rapport, trust, and respect between the people involved.

3.   Coaching takes a conscious effort, but it does not often have to be a huge investment of time.

2.   The leader may have a personal bias that his or her solution is the best, and yet the leader who chooses to coach understands that to lead means not to make others think and act as the leader does.

1.   If the reader can take nothing else from this book, it is the hope that he or she will strive to be a better listener.

SECTION I

WHAT IT IS AND WHY DO IT

The Win-Win Power of Coaching

One of the main ways that people's workdays extend from eight hours to nine hours, or nine hours to ten or eleven hours, is due to their interest in being helpful to others. This may seem counter intuitive. However, being helpful is one reason people tend to rise up in organizations. Due to our ability to do great work, we become promoted to team leader, supervisor, senior manager, department chair, or executive. We are rewarded for our ability to make decisions, solve problems, and get things done. From our positions, it feels good to help those around us. It is rewarding to assist or mentor others as they navigate their jobs and daily situations. This apparent altruistic behavior, though, can oftentimes come at a cost. Here is a specific example.

James, a research director, is leaving a meeting on one side of the building where he works. The meeting ran long, and he is rushing to get across the building to another meeting with his superiors, for which he is now fifteen minutes late. The prior meeting included some unpleasant reports that could affect James' operating budget for the next fiscal year, possibly to include cutting programs or even positions. Weighing the possibilities in his mind as he briskly walks the halls, a colleague, Kate, sees James pass her door and jumps out to stop him. "Do you have a sec?" she asks. Without stopping to think or even see who it is, James turns around, saying "What's up?"

This moment reveals James' error. He doesn't *really* have a minute, he is already late and his superiors are waiting for his status report. In addition, once he realizes it is Kate who has stopped him, his brain floods with panic as he thinks to himself,

"Oh no, it's Kate. She always rambles on and on before getting to the point! What do I do now???"

In this interaction, Kate does indeed ramble a bit, but with some prodding reveals her issue. "I have been trying to get hold of Pam from Pediatrics for a week. I sent her two emails and left a voice mail. I can't turn in that report you need by Thursday without her data! What do I do?" she stammers. In a flash James remembers that Pam is in the meeting he is on his way to now. "Pam is in my next meeting; what do you need to find out and I'll ask her" James responds. Kate is grateful for his help and provides the request.

James is now twenty minutes late for the meeting. Additionally, he now has the burden of trying to get the information Kate needs from Pam; he will need to stay after the meeting to talk about it, and then get back to Kate with the necessary information. Thus, more responsibility and work for James. What does Kate get to do? She gets to go back and get "real work" done in her office, while James does this piece of work for her!

Whose issue is this? It was and could have remained Kate's, but James just happened to be walking by, is a helpful colleague, and has access to Pam, so why not provide support to Kate? This is how a nine-hour work day becomes an eleven-hour work day; little moments such as this that pile up. In 1974, *Harvard Business Review* printed what has become one of their all-time most popular articles. Written by William Oncken, Jr. and Donald L. Wass, it was called, "Who's Got the Monkey?"[3] A simple story sums up the thrust of the article:

A manager is sitting in his office, and someone comes to the office door with a monkey on his shoulder and asks for help with a work issue. The person sits across the desk from the manager and begins explaining the situation. During the course of the conversation, the monkey crawls off the shoulder of the person, moves across the desk and up onto the shoulder of the manager. The person then leaves the manager's office. Lastly, we can see the office building at night. All the lights are off in the building, except in this one manager's office, and he is flung over his desk with monkeys all over his back.

Being helpful can correlate with taking on other people's work. How does this happen to lots of well intentioned, hard-working managers, colleagues, and executives? It starts with situations like the interaction between James and Kate.

In one small moment, James took the monkey from Kate by faltering in two ways. First, he failed to clarify immediately to Kate that he did not have a minute, as he was already running fifteen minutes late for an important meeting. Appropriate responses to Kate might have been, "I am running extremely late, but I will stop back by your office as soon as I get out of this meeting," or, "I have about thirty seconds while I walk to this meeting I am late for. Want to walk with me until I get to the conference room?"

In both of these alternatives, James would be clarifying expectations and setting appropriate boundaries with Kate. He would not be shutting her down or refusing to be helpful. Unfortunately, however, that is not what James chose to do. On the contrary, he willingly took the monkey from Kate. Essentially what he communicated to Kate was, "Give me that monkey. I'll take care of it for you!"

The second way James faltered in this case study was that he failed to recognize a stealth coaching opportunity. By rushing to "get things done," he missed the essential situation Kate was dealing with.

If James had invested a few moments with Kate, he would have found that she had not yet tried to physically seek out Pam; with a little more digging he could have discovered the true root issue: Kate is intimidated to bother or confront Pam, as she is James' boss and is two levels above her in the organizational chart. If James had discovered these key components of Kate's situation, the conversation could have looked much different. James could have helped Kate unearth her concerns about confronting Pam (and perhaps anyone of higher authority). He could have strategized with her on how to both get what she needs from Pam and how to successfully deal with superiors.

This short investment of sincere interest in Kate could have resulted in a much different result. Would James still have to devote a little time with Kate, perhaps rather than just talking to Pam himself? Yes, but Kate's growth would not have been stunted. When James took on Kate's monkey, he taught her that she can go back to him to solve her problems.

How can the cycle of dependency, illustrated by James' interaction with Kate, be broken once it is established? How can the dynamics of helping others artfully rebalance them towards self-reliance, and towards independence of thought and action? It starts with the mindset one brings to the relationship – the mindset of helping others learn how to help themselves. The tool supporting this approach is coaching.

Dog-Ear These Ideas

✓ *Notice how often you take other's work and/or responsibilities (monkeys). Use these recognitions as reminders to allow others to learn and develop.*

✓ *Be on the lookout for situations in which others are trying to give you their monkeys.*

✓ *Establish your boundaries and make them known. This is one of the healthiest behaviors you can bring to the workplace.*

✓ *Develop a mindset that to be helpful starts by not taking on others' problems.*

Why Coaching?

Empirical support for coaching comes from many sources. Perhaps the most revealing data were identified very early in coaching's foray into the workplace, in exploring how learners retain knowledge when developing new skills.[4] When knowledge-transfer processes are supported by coaching, the retention levels of newly learned skills and experiences increase dramatically:

- ✓ 5% of learners will transfer a new skill into their practice as a result of theory

- ✓ 10% will transfer a new skill into their practice with theory and demonstration

- ✓ 20% will transfer a new skill into their practice with theory, demonstration, and skill practice

- ✓ 25% will transfer a new skill into their practice with theory, demonstration, skill practice, and feedback

- ✓ **90% will transfer a new skill into their practice with theory, demonstration, skill practice, feedback, *and coaching*.**

Consider that the typical employee's knowledge transfer goes from 25% through traditional training practices to 90% with the support of coaching! Leaders cannot afford not to add this tool to their toolbox.

Furthermore, 70% of all on-the-job learning happens informally at a peer-to-peer level.[5] Coaching is an ideal vehicle for the transference of knowledge into self-supporting action – the coachee's own abilities and skills are developed, allowing them to perform at increased levels of independence. The benefits of coaching, as reported by professionals receiving it include:

✓ Enhanced sense of professional skill

✓ Increased ability to analyze his or her own processes

✓ Better understanding about best practices

✓ Wider repertoire of strategies/resources

✓ Deeper sense of purpose and meaning to his or her work

✓ Stronger professional ties with colleagues

✓ Improved performance

✓ More cohesive work culture

✓ Positive work climate.

Researcher Robert J. Menges found, for example, that teachers engaged in peer coaching reported it to be an effective tool in helping them meet their goals. Many found it comforting to see that the behavior problems they face in the classroom (e.g. students talking in class) were not unique to their classes alone. Teachers in one peer coaching program reported "increased motivation and renewed interest in teaching."[6] Thus, coaching in any relationship format (supervisor-employee, peer-to-peer, or employee-supervisor) can be a powerful tool for building the coachee's leadership acuity, confidence, and skills.

This notion is further supported by sponsored research from the International Coach Federation (ICF), the world's largest and most respected coaching organization in the world. To explore the value and impact of coaching, ICF commissioned PricewaterhouseCoopers LLP and Association Resource Centre, Inc. to conduct a global study of over 2,000 coaching clients. Results showed that for no less than 70% of those surveyed, coaching had a positive impact on clients' work performance, interpersonal and communication skills, relationships, and confidence.[7]

In this developing age of diverse, innovative, and knowledge-based workers, contemporary tools are needed to maximize talent and develop current and future leaders. Coaching has emerged as a primary instrument for this need. With strong findings to support coaching, it is very hard to overlook its value, impact, and increased use for interpersonal, performance, and workplace success.

Dog-Ear These Ideas

✓ *Reinforce any learning situation with coaching to improve learner retention and application of new skills.*

✓ *Seek opportunities to support others' learning and development.*

✓ *Foster peer (or other) group support networks to improve morale, performance, and to practice stealth coaching skills.*

What is Coaching?

The idea of coaching is not new. Upon further reading, it will become clear that these concepts, principles, and skills have actually been around for quite a long time. However, clarifying coaching's value and practicality is how it has gained traction in the workplace.

There are hundreds of different definitions of coaching; each articulating what coaching is from its own unique context (such as coaching in athletics, coaching for graduate school dissertation preparation, or coaching artists and singers). Having a universal understanding of coaching can be muddy at best. However, certain principles to coaching seem to be common, and for leaders, one is that coaching focuses on fostering others' leadership capabilities.

> *For leaders charged with maximizing performance and results (for themselves and the organization), coaching is the process of helping people focus, discover, and/or clarify: (1) where they are today, (2) where they want to go, and (3) how to get there.*

> *That is, coaching is primarily a present and future focused tool for expanding others' leadership abilities.*

> *Coaching relies heavily on:*

> ✓ *The belief that others have the ability to develop and work through their own solutions (thus the coach tempers his/her own desire to provide solutions).*

> ✓ *The skills of conscious listening.*

> ✓ *The use of quality questions to drive the conversation forward towards action.*

Let's explore this definition further. First and foremost, coaching in the workplace is about helping others be the best they can be. Ultimately this fuels a more effective and efficient workforce, getting things done with maximized quality and sustainability for the long haul. There are numerous other tools to build teams, overcome differences, or improve emotional intelligence. However, a big part of the leader's role is the accomplishment of goals and objectives in support of the organization's mission. Coaching leverages and unleashes peoples' innate talent and desire towards this purpose.

Going back to the case study on James and Kate (chapter 1, The Win-Win Power of Coaching), James could have used coaching techniques, shaping the conversation this way:

> James: What is your main cause for concern with this, Kate?
>
> Kate: I can't get the information I need from Pam, and I am running out of time.
>
> James: What have you tried so far?
>
> Kate: I have emailed three times and called twice. I left a voice mail message both times. I don't want to appear too needy, but the data she has is vital.
>
> James: Sounds like you have been working hard to reach her. Is there anything you haven't tried yet?
>
> Kate: Well, I haven't physically gone to her office.
>
> James: What has kept you from trying that strategy?
>
> Kate: Like I said, I don't want to appear like an annoyance to her. She's your boss, James. I bet she doesn't even know what I do.
>
> James: Let me make sure I am hearing you correctly. You have tried numerous times to reach Pam, to no avail. And you are hesitating to approach her in person because you don't want to be a pain in the rear end. Is that right?
>
> Kate: Yes, that's right.

James: I think I may also be hearing that you haven't taken all the steps you could – trying to get her when she is in her office. Is that right?

Kate: Um... yes, I guess so.

James: What is your hesitancy in going to her office?

Kate: I am intimidated. She is the "big boss" around here!

James: Ah, ok, I could see how that can be intimidating. You know, Kate, you are fully capable of handling a conversation with Pam.

Kate: Really? No way... You think so?

James: Definitely. And I can understand wanting to feel fully ready for that conversation. I have to get to my meeting, but in the meantime, how about putting a meeting on our calendars for us to plan for how you can have this conversation with Pam?

Kate: What do you mean?

James: I mean at my next one-on-one with Pam, I am happy to bring you along so you have access to Pam. But before that, we need to meet and prepare how to have that conversation. How does that sound to you?

Kate: Makes me nervous. But I do need to talk to her.

James: I understand. First time I had a meeting with the CEO, I thought I was going to be sick, I was so nervous! But you know what? She is just a person trying to get work done, just like you and me. I've got to run, but before we meet, think about what you want from Pam and how you would like the conversation to go. See you soon!

In this short example, with a conversation that may take a minute or less, James moves Kate from her current state to a future state, along with a plan of action – a time to meet with Pam and a meeting to prepare for the engagement. This is a distinguishing factor of coaching conversations versus other types of interactions. In coaching, the coach is consciously working to move the coachee into actions towards a preferred future state.

Coaching is thus a "process" rather than a model. There is no clearly defined path or structure to follow. The coach cannot finish a coaching conversation and say to the coachee, "Okay, I did these four steps and asked these twelve questions. Good, you have now been coached. Now get out of my office and go succeed." (Of course, the coach could say these things, yet the result may not be what was intended.) Rather, coaching is fluid, and the coach must be willing to be flexible, while still moving the conversation towards action.

When coaching someone, the coachee may be in various states of readiness for coaching. Perhaps the coachee is clear on his or her situation and possible courses of action, and needs the coach's help to focus on which strategy is best to take. However, the coachee may have no idea what to do as of yet, and may be looking to the coach for help or solutions. In this case, the coachee needs to gain more clarity about his or her situation first, prior to considering options or actions. Many times, simply verbalizing one's thoughts and feelings is enough for the coachee to gain a new perspective on the situation, as we saw in the coaching conversation between James and Kate. In addressing a few simple questions, Kate's awareness was raised to the true issue at hand, her fear of approaching senior management.

Perhaps a most distinguishable factor from other types of communication tools is that coaching is a present and future-focused conversation. Coaching has a bias for moving towards preferred future states and exploring the action steps necessary to reach desired outcomes. Coaching only explores the past to gain insight into ineffective past strategies or clarify some context. Coaching is conversation to move the coachee into action. The action may not occur after one conversation, but the goal of coaching is to escort someone from where they are to where they want or need to be.

For example, in the story above, James was able to recognize Kate's efforts early on, and utilize it as a way to turn the conversation towards coaching when he said, "Sounds like you have been working hard to reach her. Is there anything you haven't tried yet?"

Essentially what James has done in one sentence is to imply, "You have tried this and that a thousand times, and it's not working. Let's leave that and explore what else could be done here."

This is where the coaching mindset comes in to play. In choosing to coach, James' desire is to develop Kate's own leadership skill set. The leader is supporting the coachee in developing her own processing, analysis, problem solving, decision making, strategizing, or other leader acumen relevant to the issue at hand. To create the environment for this mindset to exist, the coaching leader must be willing to allow the coachee space to think and problem solve, without offering solutions.

> *A fundamental assumption imbedded in coaching is that people have the innate ability to solve their own problems. The coaching leader provides the context for the coachee to do just that.*

Furthermore, the effectiveness of coaching can be directly related to the quality of the coach's listening. What distinguishes conscious listening from active listening or listening for information? It is the depth of the listening intention. In coaching it means being attentive to what the person is saying (words), as well as how he or she is experiencing the situation being described (perspective). This type of listening involves a heightened state of awareness, an inquisitive mind, and a patient temperament.

If conscious listening establishes the coaching base, the main driver in moving coaching conversations forward towards action is inquiry. Quality questions lead to quality answers and heightened self-referral by the coachee. The generation of effective coaching questions comes from good listening. In fact, during a coaching conversation, the next "right" question for the coach emerges, rather than being planned.

Conscious listening and framing quality questions will be explored in chapters eleven and twelve.

Dog-Ear These Ideas

- ✓ *Provide support by helping others learn to solve their own problems, not by solving other people's problems for them.*

- ✓ *Maintain the belief that the coachee has the answers within him or herself.*

- ✓ *Listen carefully. It provides a roadmap of what to explore, and informs the development of quality questions.*

- ✓ *Ask questions to expand the coachee's thinking beyond his or her current capacity and to move him or her toward a plan of action.*

- ✓ *Temper the desire to provide advice.*

What is Stealth Coaching?

Similar to other models of coaching, stealth coaching is a simple dialogue process that helps individuals tap into their own innate reflection, critical thinking, and problem-solving capabilities. It is a method to gently engage others through inquiry, encouraging them to reflect more and broaden their understanding of themselves and their unique abilities. There is no magic to stealth coaching. As opposed to more formal coaching, stealth coaching can easily be incorporated into everyday conversations.

When one begins to integrate stealth coaching into everyday conversations, though, people might be a bit shocked. If people are used to receiving answers, solutions, suggestions, and direction, to suddenly experience deep listening, focus, and lots of questions from the leader can be surprising and uncomfortable. The knee-jerk reaction by most is to resist the leader's new techniques. How does the leader introduce these skills to the workforce, then, without having them be immediately rejected? For many, starting a potential coaching conversation with "I've just learned these new skills, so how about I *coach* you through this situation?" is a surefire recipe for disaster in one's workplace. So what else can be done?

To be stealthful is to be subtle, patient and still, while at the same time actively scanning the environment for coaching opportunities, much like what might be seen in a kung fu movie starring Bruce Lee. One can imagine Lee entering a courtyard slowly, quietly, and with heightened attentiveness to his surroundings. His personal "radar" always seems to be up and in full operation.

Stealth coaching starts with this heightened state of awareness. Then:

1. *Identify a development opportunity, in the moment.*

2. *Recognize when the situation is, in fact, an opportunity to utilize coaching versus other development tools.*

3. *Stealthfully move the conversation into a coaching framework.*

Here is an example of how this can be done:

Carolyn is a senior manager in a well-known federal agency. She has thirteen direct reports, most of them supervisors, and a total of 121 employees working under her. One of her reports, Frank, is bright, talented, and eager to succeed. He aspires to move up to an executive level position as fast as he can. Frank is a good performer but is young, both in age and experience, and needs to mature further as a supervisor and a leader. He believes he is capable of doing more than what his current role allows.

Carolyn and Frank have talked in circles numerous times about his eagerness and his competence as a technical supervisor and a leader of people. Carolyn believes that he has been growing impatient with what he perceives as her "holding him back" from doing more. Carolyn recognizes his talent but can't seem to shake the pattern she is in with him: he comes to her with ideas and she constantly shoots them down. The conversations typically end up with Carolyn telling Frank what to do, followed by a long explanation and rationalization as to why he needs to do the task as she describes. As a result, Frank experiences being stifled, and Carolyn experiences frustration at trying to "tame a wild horse."

Last week, Carolyn's boss gave her division a new project to work on. Carolyn recognized that the work was a good fit for Frank, but she was concerned he would rush too quickly to complete it and would miss many complexities imbedded in this kind of project. Rather than direct Frank on what steps to take,

> Carolyn recognized this new project as an opportunity to try coaching him instead.
>
> At their regularly scheduled one-on-one meeting that week, Carolyn introduced the project assignment to Frank. He seemed excited by the new opportunity and immediately jumped into brainstorming implementation ideas. Carolyn could see his blind spots and potential pit falls in the many project components he was not recognizing. She felt her frustration and her blood pressure rise, as it had many times in this type of situation with Frank. However, this time she chose to try a different strategy, a stealth coaching approach.
>
> "I like your ideas and enthusiasm, Frank," Carolyn said. "This is a big opportunity for you and your team. My boss and the Congressional Subcommittee will be watching closely on this one. There are a lot of moving parts. Why don't we take some time to walk through this together?"
>
> Rather than telling Frank how to tackle the project, Carolyn had opened a different door with Frank, a subtle opportunity for them to engage differently.
>
> "What do you mean?" replied Frank.
>
> "Well, tell me what you see as the core issues of this assignment," Carolyn clarified.

In that moment, rather than Carolyn instructing Frank on what *she* saw as the core issues and the strategies to take, she provided the space for *Frank* to do the thinking, and ultimately, with her support, to do the strategizing as well.

Turning everyday conversations towards stealth coaching involves being gentle at first, noticing one's own impulses to tell rather than to ask, and to adjust the discussion to one of inquiry. When Carolyn adopted this style of interaction with Frank, she broke through the former conflicting dynamic with her employee, transforming their discussion to one focused on productive outcomes.

Dog-Ear These Ideas

✓ *Keep your "antennae" up for coachable moments.*

✓ *Be ready for opportunities to coach at teachable moments versus just during supervisory or performance review sessions.*

✓ *Use your desire to provide answers as a personal signal to begin stealth coaching instead.*

✓ *Notice when others resist your advice. This may indicate a good time to stealth coach.*

How Does Stealth Coaching Differ from Other Forms of Coaching?

The key factors that differentiate stealth coaching from other forms of coaching are (1) who uses it, and (2) the way it is implemented.

Stealth coaching is a tool for workplace success, and, importantly, it can be used by *anyone* in the organization, regardless of job title, role, or position. It is one of many options a leader can use at appropriate times, as stealth coaching is a situational device to be used in informal, fluid ways. Thus the use of stealth coaching can be implemented as needs present themselves or opportunities warrant.

Not every conversation is a stealth coaching opportunity, however. In fact, many are not. Most conversations are routine in nature: conveying information, sharing stories, answering customer questions, enforcing policies, etc. How then does the leader differentiate situations and conversations to recognize stealth coaching opportunities?

Refer to the following chart to distinguish between different types of coaching, based on their definition and use, as well as length of time each is typically utilized in applicable relationships.

Coaching Type	Definition	Length of Relationship
Athletic Coaching	Perhaps the most commonly identified use of coaching. In this setting, the coach assumes many roles: team manager, recruiter, teacher, motivator, disciplinarian, mentor, and decision maker. Coaches can be volunteers, interns, students, or professionals, depending on the nature of the sporting activity.	Coaching relationship lasts as long as the two are working together, though in some cases the connection may be maintained even after one or the other has left the shared team or sport.
Executive Coaching	A formalized, contracted relationship between a professional coach and a client (executive or manager typically) who desires the service; identified by clearly defined roles, timelines, goals and expectations for outcomes. The coach charges fees for this service.	The length of engagement is contracted. Any continuation of the coaching relationship is determined through re-contracting. The coach-coachee relationship may be short (a few conversations), or longer, depending on the complexity of the client's needs.
Training Program Coaching	Coaching to support participants in management or leadership training programs; provided to participants to support their learning or to explore the results of personality or performance feedback instruments. Coaches may be internal employees to the organization, or external coaches may be contracted to deliver the service.	This relationship is typically limited in nature — one conversation, a prescribed number of sessions/hours, or coaching throughout the length of the program.

Coaching Type	Definition	Length of Relationship
Peer Coaching	An informal relationship (typically) between colleagues, in which each person is open to both coaching and being coached by the other(s). Frequently mentoring (see below) may be used as part of peer coaching.	Lasts as long as warranted. Peer coaches can work together for extended periods, take time off, reconvene, or only meet once. The length of the peer coaching relationship is based on the needs of each person, shared interest, timing, and availability.
Mentoring	A formal or informal relationship between a person wanting to learn a skill, trade, process, or other specific item for knowledge transfer and the subject matter expert who provides the information. A mentor may or may not use coaching techniques as part of the mentoring process. Mentors can come from personal and professional contexts and usually are not paid a fee to act as a mentor.	Varies depending on the mentoring topic's complexity. The best mentoring relationships typically develop naturally. In formal and informal situations, the mentoring relationship lasts until the mentee has learned what he or she needs and is ready to move on.
Stealth Coaching	An informal communication process between two people that can be utilized in almost any context where the coachee has a situation in which more than one solution is possible. There are no fees associated with stealth coaching.	Length of relationship is irrelevant in the context of stealth coaching. A person utilizing stealth coaching techniques can utilize the skills in both short and long-term relationships.

Dog-Ear These Ideas

✓ *Learn to distinguish among various types and contexts of coaching. Coaching for executives or managers is very different from coaching in athletics, which is different from peer coaching or coaching as a mentor.*

✓ *Recognize that many conversations are not coachable moments, and that teaching, informing, brain storming, or the like may be more appropriate.*

✓ *Add stealth coaching into almost any workplace context to move the conversation from a one way transaction – telling – to a dialogue between people.*

✓ *Coaching (in any form) is not therapy. Therapy helps people work through mental or psychological issues, typically grown out of their <u>past</u> histories, which affect their ability to have healthy functioning lives. Coaching is a present and <u>future</u>-focused tool to maximize people's performance, skills, and abilities.*

What Are Noticeable Results of Stealth Coaching?

It may be difficult to spot indicators of success when beginning to utilize stealth coaching in the workplace. Coaching is not telling, so the coach may not see instantaneous results as when using traditional directing or problem-solving tools. However, if the coach remains patient and observant, powerful results will soon emerge.

Perhaps the most poignant example may be the employee who comes to his or her manager seeking help. If the manager chooses to take a mindset of resolving and solution giving, this choice begins the cycle of dependency. However, by taking a coaching stance, the employee's behavior changes noticeably and sustainably and dependency lessens. The employee soon begins to come to the manager with issues but also brings an idea or two on how to resolve the situation. With more coaching, the manager notices that the employee shows up less frequently with issues and more often with strategies and options. As the employee's self-sufficiency and problem solving acuity continue to prosper, one day the interaction between the two may look like this:

The employee knocks on the manager's door and says, "Hey Boss, we have a 'fire' going on." The employee explains it clearly and succinctly and follows it up with, "I've been giving it some thought and I have four possible solutions... here is the one I think we should go with and why." The employee concludes by stating, "I have completed the paperwork for you and all you need to do is sign off. I have also typed up a sample email for you to send to the appropriate stakeholders, informing them of what is occurring and the steps we are taking."

This is a radical yet realistic notion of employee development. Accompanying an employee as he or she moves from potential capabilities to fully developed abilities includes the exploration of the employee's habits, mental barriers, and leadership mindset. Revealing untapped potential in someone can be a daunting task to undertake, yet it is attainable when approached strategically and artfully. Most people want to learn and grow, and the results of allowing space for that is remarkable.

Other indicators the coach may expect to see are included in the following chart:

Change or Result	Measure
Changes in attitude and/or behavior.	*The coachee is performing in new ways.*
Fewer complaints of feeling stuck.	*The coachee seeks to be rescued less and less.*
The coach gets fewer routine problems and more quality issues coming to him or her.	*The coachee is more adept at handling his or her own situations and is working more strategically.*
Improved rapport and trust.	*The coachee is willing to disclose more to the coach, and both coach and coachee see one another as more capable in their roles.*
Increased capacity to solve one's own problems.	*The coach has more time to do his or her own work, as the coachee is working with increased independence.*
More positive outlook.	*The coachee has a changed mindset that is reflected in relationships with others.*
Increased ownership in finding solutions.	*The coachee is proactive, self-sufficient, and problem-solving rather than reactive and incapable.*

Change or Result	Measure
Others seek more conversations with the stealth coaching leader.	*As the coachee comes to appreciate the coach's way of interacting (deep listening and solution-driven inquiry), the coachee returns to fine tune strategies and further develop leadership capacities.*
Coachee demonstrates increased self-referring behavior.	*Recognition of challenges and ownership of changes.*
Team operates at a higher level.	*The team becomes empowered, working more independently and productively.*
Willingness to explore different perspectives.	*This is perhaps the most vital component of the change process. The coachee's development can be correlated to receptivity to feedback, openness to exploring other options, and inclination to make adjustments to him or herself.*

Dog-Ear These Ideas

✓ Be patient. Seeing the effects of coaching can sometimes take time, but the results are worth it.

✓ Once you commit to coaching, look for success indicators in the coachee (see chart above for examples).

✓ Once you commit to coaching, look for success indicators for yourself:

- Others are less dependent on you for solutions.

- In emails, you are moved more frequently from the "To:" line to the "CC:" line (or perhaps off the email chain entirely).

- You have more time freed up to focus on other aspects of your work.

✓ Once you commit to coaching, look for success indictors in the organization:

- Employee retention and morale increases.

- Cultivation of informal peer coaching and mentoring grows.

- Organizational succession planning and "bench strength" increases.

- Your team can perform well with or without your presence.

Coaching vs. Mentoring

Confusion can result from the lack of distinction between what a coach does and what a mentor does. To best understand these differences, it can be useful to understand the root of each. Mentoring and coaching evolved from two very different places.

Mentoring has its roots in Greek mythology. Upon leaving for the Trojan War, Odysseus, King of Ithaca (and central character in Homer's epic tale, *The Odyssey*), asks his good friend, Mentor, to look after his son, Telemachus, in his absence. Odysseus was gone for approximately ten years, leaving Mentor with great responsibility for the care and guidance of Telemachus.

Mentoring today is typically viewed as the imparting of wisdom, knowledge, and influence by one who is more experienced to one who is less experienced. A mentor is often an expert in a specific area (such as technical expertise, career experience, or political savvy and knowledge) who imparts his or her wisdom to the mentee with less experience or knowledge in that area.

In contrast to mentoring, coaching has its origins in psychology and the fundamental belief that people innately have the ability to solve their own problems. Wilhelm Wundt (1832-1920), regarded by many as the founder of psychology as an academic discipline, believed that psychology is based on the observation of experience.[8] Wundt's work is the basis for contemporary self-referral, or looking at our own thoughts and behaviors as the basis for changes we may want to make in ourselves or the way we engage with the outer world.

Later in the 20th century, Wolfgang Kohler (1887-1967) became known for his work on the topic of problem solving. Perhaps his most famous study involved an ape named Sultan. Kept in a cage,

Sultan was given two hollow bamboo sticks. A banana was placed outside the cage, out of the ape's range. He failed at multiple attempts to reach the banana with the sticks. At a certain point Sultan was observed to sit for a period of time, quietly, after which he connected the two sticks together and was able to reach the banana. Kohler called the sudden solution that followed the ape's quiet time "insight;" and asserted that insight was at the root of problem solving.

What Wundt and Kohler uncovered in their research is the truism that one can become, upon reflection, a better thinker and problem-solver. Out of this premise, coaching evolved as a vehicle, a process, to help individuals tap into their innate reflective, improvement, and problem-solving capabilities.

For someone to be effective as a coach, he or she needs *not* be an expert on the topic the coachee confronts. The coach, through intentional and structured use of listening and inquiry, is the catalyst to unlock the coachee's own thinking.

A mentor, on the other hand, may use the skills of coaching when mentoring someone, though it is not necessary for the mentor to do so. Conversely, a coach does not have to be a mentor to effectively use coaching skills to help someone. The two are distinct, as shown below:

Mentor	Coach
Is a subject matter expert	Is not necessarily a subject matter expert
Provides advice, experience, and expertise	Provides a process for the coachee to think about his or her situation more clearly and to strategize options and solutions
Is more apt to give solutions	Is more apt to ask questions

Mentor	Coach
May ask questions to help formulate advice	Will ask questions to broaden the coachee's understanding of and possibilities for handling the situation
Can utilize the skills of coaching as a tool in the mentoring process	Will typically refrain from advising in order that the coachee maintain issue ownership

Dog-Ear These Ideas

✓ *When you are asked to be a mentor, know that you have been chosen for your expertise, experience, or network of connections.*

✓ *Recognize when you are in a mentor role and look for opportunities to use stealth coaching to support or enhance your teaching and advisement.*

✓ *To clarify when and how coaching can be utilized, encourage your organization's human resources and/or training office to better educate the organization on the differences between coaching and mentoring.*

✓ *When coaching, allow the coachee time to think. Quiet reflection is appropriate and normal when coaching. The coachee may be formulating a great method to "reach the banana!"*

The Business Case to Be a Coaching Leader

As a leader, one may now have these questions about the need to become a coach. What does it do for the leader? Why bother? How does it help the actual business?

In 2006, the Center for Creative Leadership (CCL), routinely ranked as one of the top ten sources for executive education in the world, began a study on "The Stress of Leadership." CCL surveyed their program graduates, mostly middle and upper level managers and executives, to identify key areas that bring stress at work.

One question asked was, "What are the leadership demands that cause stress?" The top three most frequent responses to this question were: (1) demands on resources and time, (2) developing others, and (3) establishing and maintaining relationships. Leading others demands both time and the willingness to give effort to influencing and guiding.[9] Being a leader is hard work!

A second key question from the CCL study was, "How do your direct reports contribute to your stress?" The single highest reply (nearly 50% of all respondents) noted "personal accountability;" if employees would only do their jobs, maintain a decent standard of quality, attempt to manage and solve their own problems, make appropriate decisions (and the list could go on), the leader's job would be exponentially less stressful. Ultimately, the CCL study revealed that:

> *A workforce lacking in self-reliance, critical thinking acumen and the ability to work strategically greatly impacts its dependency on the leader.*

Given this reality of workplace stress, the leader is left with two key issues to confront. The first issue concerns the leader's own mindset.

How does the leader see and perceive challenges with employees? The leader's attitude affects how he or she will interact with followers. The second issue concerns development. Exactly how can the leader increase the number of independent, high-performing employees while reducing their dependency on the leader?

Skillfully addressing these two issues can be daunting. A study by the Gallup organization, across business sectors, found that a mere 33% of the workforce is engaged, being productive, timely, efficient, and effective in their jobs. Gallup found 49% of the workforce to be unengaged, and an alarming 18% to be "actively disengaged," or not bought in to their work, role, and/or the mission of the organization.[10] The result is that nearly a fifth of the workforce is consciously making decisions to do other things besides be productive at work.

As Daniel Pink acknowledges in *Drive: The Surprising Truth about What Motivates Us*, there must be better solutions for inspiring our workforces other than the timeworn stick and carrot methods of cash awards and bonuses.[11] People want to contribute, if only given engaging opportunities to do so. Economic studies have found that employees no longer respond well to these old motivational strategies in a knowledge-based work environment, where the job requires more than basic cognitive skills.[12] Additionally, people are drawn to perform at higher and higher levels not as a result of salary, but as a result of having opportunities to be self-directed, to improve their skills and knowledge, and to make a meaningful contribution.[13]

What strategies exist, then, for leaders to engage employees who are motivated by opportunities for self-directed skill enhancement and meaningful work? Why would they trust and follow a leader towards these new realities? What leadership qualities help keep employees engaged, in the post carrot-and-stick environment? What kind of leaders do employees follow and trust?

Though conducted more than twenty years ago, James Kouzes and Barry Posner's research on trusted leaders still provides us relevant clarity today as to how the leader can effectively engage his or her workers. The study, conducted over a period of fifteen years, consisted of interviews with more than 20,000 people in America, Asia,

Europe, and Australia. It was looking for common themes to a basic survey question: "What values (personal traits or characteristics) do you look for and admire in your superiors?" Findings are below: [14]

Characteristic	% of People Surveyed Who Admire This Characteristic
Honest	88
Forward Thinking	75
Inspiring	68
Competent	63
Fair-Minded	49
Supportive	41
Broad-minded	40
Intelligent	40
Straightforward	33
Dependable	32

What immediately jumps out when analyzing these findings is that the top three items are more about engaging people, rather than being technically savvy or having the right letters after one's name. In fact, across cultures and business sectors, Kouzes and Posner found that more than anything we simply want our leaders to tell us the truth. Would it not be refreshing if an organization's leadership admitted when they made a mistake or owned up when they did not know the answer?

The challenge of effective leadership does not lie in technical expertise or having all the answers, but in fundamental human decency, and in getting out of the way to allow for others' potential to grow and flourish.

(In the chart above, it is also interesting how far down on the list intelligence falls. Apparently, one does not have to have a very high IQ to be viewed as a good leader.)

The leader who chooses to coach understands that he or she is in the relationship business. To be successful, the leader must rely on others, and human beings are funny creatures. They have values, assumptions, beliefs, goals, and expectations. When the leader can meet them where they are and help open their potential, a win-win occurs for all parties. Coaching is perhaps the most important resource the leader can use to realize this possibility.

Dog-Ear These Ideas

✓ *Embrace the notion that leading is a relationship business.*

✓ *Explore how coaching is a primary driver for building relationships and developing talent.*

✓ *Observe those who are effective at building relationships and seek to become skilled with those techniques.*

✓ *Admit mistakes and uncertainties. It is the simplest and most powerful way to be perceived as honest, trustworthy, and competent – fundamental components to gaining followers and opening them up to being coached.*

✓ *Find healthy ways to improve your relationship with stress. Try exercise, meditation, gardening, journaling, or other activities. De-stressing is vital for healthy and helpful interactions with others.*

SECTION II

HOW IT WORKS

The Coaching Mindset: How Mentality Influences Choices, Actions, and Outcomes

A rock pile ceases to be a rock pile the moment a single person contemplates it, bearing within the image of a cathedral.[15]

The notion above, adapted from author Antoine de Saint Exupery, describes the mentality of looking for coachable moments over other forms of communication or engagement. Coaching is successful when the coach sees possibility in the coachee. Whereas others may only see a pile of rocks, or cannot see what potential lies before them, the coach chooses to look for potential, the cathedral within the rock pile. If one can only see limitations in life, most likely that person will experience a life of restrictions.

Consider the teacher, mentor, friend, or supervisor who sees more in a person than the person sees in him or herself. Great influences in life often come from people who push a person beyond what they can see or thought was possible. The impact of such relationships can be life-long. Many of us have people who have powerfully shaped our lives – instilling confidence, pride, determination, and values that have carried us through many challenges.

This gift of visioning and encouragement, provided by others who see us as more than a pile of rocks, is derived from the mindset of possibility. Possibility is a theme we can routinely spot in life and in the workplace. For example:

Douglas McGregor was the President of Antioch College from 1948 to 1954 and later joined the faculty of MIT's Sloan School of Management. His most prominent work was his 1960 book, *The Human Side of Enterprise*, which outlined his theory that there are two main ways in which managers (leaders) can view the workforce around them. McGregor described two mental constructs that influence managers' workplace behaviors. He called these descriptions Theory X and Theory Y.[16] Today we might call them "Coaching Leaders versus Command and Control Management."

Command and Control Managers assume that others:

✓ Have a genuine distaste for work

✓ Must be prodded, coerced, or threatened into work because it is so unpleasant

✓ Prefer to be closely supervised

✓ Avoid as much responsibility as they can

✓ Have little ambition

✓ Value security above all else.

Coaching Leaders assume that others:

✓ Want to work because working is natural

✓ Will exercise self-control if they are committed to the results to be achieved

✓ Will be motivated to achieve goals if they value the goals

✓ Share imagination and creativity – traits that are not limited solely to management

✓ Are "boxed in" by job descriptions and are capable of realizing more potential than they are typically given a chance to do.

Those who have a Command and Control ideology view the world and those surrounding them as problems to be controlled; they find the world and its people untrustworthy. This viewpoint creates natural obstacles that oftentimes limit the leader's capabilities. Such a leader might think: "Life is tough, and I need to use a hammer to beat it down." Imagine the attitude of followers when a manager attempts to lead through this lens of awareness. What are the short and long-term ramifications of utilizing this framework in today's workplace?

By contrast, the Coaching Leader ideology is one of possibility. This viewpoint creates space for followers to utilize their strengths. The Coaching Leader encourages followers to know it is okay to take risks and fail, as it is a great way to learn. The coaching mindset creates the potential for building and sustaining committed followers. Furthermore, the Coaching Leader may do as much following as leading, since he or she has created an environment filled with leaders at all levels. As Rosamund Stone Zander and Benjamin Zander state in *The Art of Possibility*:

> *Many of the circumstances that seem to block us in our daily lives may only appear to do so based on a framework of assumptions we carry with us. Draw a different frame around the same set of circumstances and new pathways come into view. Find the right framework and extraordinary accomplishment becomes an everyday experience.*[17]

Ultimately, then, the leader's mindset can open up the potential to change from one way of thinking and behaving to another.

From Command and Control	To the Coaching Leader
Reacts to crisis and past mistakes	Envisions future potential and aligns efforts around it
Pushes others to overcome weaknesses	Encourages people to develop talents and strengths
Steps in to solve others' problems	Helps people learn to identify, solve, and prevent problems
Sees managing as "what I do"	Recognizes leading as "who I am"

This change in ideology from Theory X to Theory Y has the power to transform workplace cultures, unleashing talent and fostering true employee engagement toward the organization's core mission.

McGregor's work, though developed fifty years ago, stands exceptionally relevant in today's booming information and technology age. The mindset of possibility that McGregor defined as Theory Y is a leadership attitude critical to engaging employees and motivating them to reach their highest potential. And coaching is the premier tool for becoming such a leader.

Dog-Ear These Ideas

✓ *Analyze your own leadership style to determine how much you look at your circumstances through the lens of possibility versus "do it my way."*

✓ *Challenge your assumptions when you judge a person's performance or capabilities. Ask, "Do I believe this to be true, or am I being fogged by my biases?"*

✓ *To develop self-referral skills and adjust your mindset, every day as you walk into your workplace ask yourself, "How am I showing up today?" Am I energetic, positive, enthusiastic? What am I projecting?*

✓ *Choose Coaching Leader behaviors, and consider the consequences of falling into old-school Command and Control Management styles. Do not be restricted to only your unconscious patterns of choice.*

Mindfulness Affects Attention and Focus

In 1988, Chris Melissinos stared at the hurdle that was his high school graduation. For this high-energy kid who was enrolled in gifted student programs in his home state of New York, his family's move to Virginia during his high school years proved to be largely disruptive. Chris discovered that he had increasing difficulty focusing in class, studying, and taking tests. Later in life he was diagnosed with Attention Deficit Disorder (ADD), but at the time he was in high school, the system was not diagnosing kids very often. So Chris struggled to pay attention in school, but he excelled at the things he loved – video games, programming, and science.

After struggling but graduating from high school, Chris took a sales job at a store in the local shopping mall. There he met a young woman and fell in love. She told him that he needed to go to college and tap into his potential. He agreed, and she transferred to attend school with him. Starting in community college and then finishing with high marks and a BS in Public Administration from a highly regarded university, this woman proved to be the spark that helped propel his future and career. Not long after graduation, they were married and started their life together.

During this time, Chris got a job as a sales support representative at Sun Microsystems. He excelled in this environment that encouraged exploration, technology development, and the rapidly emerging World Wide Web. He quickly rose through the ranks, first as a sales manager, then as a channel marketing manager. What happened next would propel his lifelong love of video games towards his future career.

Chris recognized that Sun, at the forefront of the growth of the Internet, was missing a huge opportunity in the rapidly expanding world of online games and video game adoption. So he drafted a very robust business plan, detailing why Sun Microsystems should jump into the video game market. He shared it with his supervisor, who was supportive and who encouraged him to share it further up the organization. However, the further up the management chain he went, the more his idea was met with resistance. Sun was plenty successful in making and selling servers and software for the Internet; video games would be a distraction, he was told. Undeterred, Chris continued talking with management further and further up the organization ladder, facing rejection after rejection.

After a year and a half of trying unsuccessfully to persuade his management chain to understand the opportunity that the multi-billion dollar video game industry represented to Sun, he decided that to truly have his idea heard, he needed to go straight to the CEO. Chris' approach was to connect with those who were sympathetic to his cause. One such person was the CEO's executive assistant. After months of trying to meet with the CEO, Chris jokingly stated to the executive assistant that if the only time the CEO had in his schedule was walking down the hall to the bathroom, he would gladly meet him then. Fortunately, she was able to arrange for a quick phone call instead.

During that fateful call, Chris explained the opportunity video games would represent for Sun in all areas of the company's developed technology. The CEO initially showed reluctance, but Chris pushed back with facts and information. The two went back and forth discussing Sun's position, the competitive landscape, application of technologies, as well as what success would look like. After a year and a half of rejection, Chris's voice and vision was not only being heard, but considered. Three weeks later, Chris was appointed the Business Development Manager for Media and Entertainment.

He became a driving force behind establishing Java as a viable technology for cross platform game development. Chris was eventually appointed Sun's "Chief Gaming Officer" and ultimately their "Chief Evangelist," touring the world and speaking at conferences and expos. Fast Company magazine included him on the short list for their annual "Fast 50" movers and shakers. Chris was living his dream, marrying the young woman who helped him find his potential, raising a beautiful family, and building their dream home. Life was sweet.

Then, in 2009 it was announced that Sun Microsystems was to be bought out by Oracle. Oracle's mission in no way included the video game industry, and Chris was informed that opportunities for him in the company would no longer include video games. He decided to leave the company in the wake of the acquisition, take some time off, and focus on his next endeavors. His experience at Sun and his clear pursuit of his passions would help lead him to one of the greatest achievements of his professional career.

In early 2009, Chris was one of only twenty senior technologists invited to attend an event called Smithsonian 2.0. The Smithsonian Institute was exploring new ways to reach the public through technology. It was here that Chris met representatives from the Smithsonian American Art Museum, and they started a conversation about video games and art. Seeds were laid that ultimately grew into an opportunity for Chris to curate the very first video game art show at the Smithsonian. In March 2012, "The Art of Video Games" exhibition opened to the world; it has become one of the most successful exhibitions in the museum's history.

How did all of this happen? What was Chris doing right? Does he have some special gift? How was Chris so successful?

Chris was not simply a video game junkie who followed his passion. He was focused and intentional in his strategy to achieve his vision. Having the capacity to give one's attention to something or someone, in a meaningful way and by choice, is the basis of mindfulness. To understand Chris's story more fully, the opposite situation, or *mindlessness*, needs to be understood.

The experience of driving an automobile while daydreaming and suddenly "waking up," noticing having travelled without being fully aware of it, is an example of mindlessness. Forgetting details of a recent conversation with a colleague, eating a meal without considering what or how much is being consumed, and judging someone's personality without knowing the person, all exemplify the mindlessness that fills everyday life.

A child learns how to tie her shoe laces. At first it can be very slow and laborious. The child's motor skills and discomfort with the new activity make it a challenging experience. A few years later, the same child can slide into shoes and tie the laces seemingly unconsciously. The task has become comfortable and routine. Little if any new mental or physical energy is needed to complete the task. The child has become unconsciously competent at tying shoe laces. Her shoe-tying has become mindless.

As we grow into adulthood, this learning pattern allows us to focus on situations that require a heightened sense of awareness and attentiveness, more brain power, or a different set of motor skills. The same is true in the workplace, where people need a context of possibility to be mindful, engaged, and motivated. People can become bored if they are no longer challenged, stimulated, or believe their work does not make a difference. In fact, it has become more and more evident that an increasing percentage of the workforce looks for career changes when there are no longer "opportunities to learn and grow."[18]

The challenge becomes keeping a workforce "awake," intrigued, and dedicated to give high quality effort and to grow professionally. What does it look like, then, when organizations are succeeding at meeting these workforce expectations?

In 2010, the Nuclear Regulatory Commission (NRC) was cited as the best place to work in the U.S. federal government.[19] One might not instinctively think of the NRC this way, but the agency actually has a growing history of very high employee satisfaction on measures such as empowerment, fairness, performance-based rewards and advancement, and training and development. CNN ranked Google as the best company to work for in 2012, as employees glow about its mission, culture, and perks.[20] In both organizational settings, public sector and corporate, salary is not the biggest factor of job satisfaction; workplace satisfaction and opportunities are. Did Chris have this same sense of opportunity at Sun?

Looking at Chris' story, it is evident that he had a goal, a mission. His attentiveness, awareness, and alertness to situations, circumstances, and corporate politics helped him make choices that led to success, both for him and for the organizations he served. Maintaining this quality of heightened awareness for a year and half, as he did to finally reach the company president, is only the beginning of his concentrated mindfulness. Once he became the Chief Gaming Officer and Chief Evangelist, the "real" work of developing Sun's video gaming operation began. Later, with his role at the Smithsonian, Chris had to maintain his sharp focus and awareness.

To clarify, to be focused on a task, situation, or issue does not mean to be obsessively engaged solely with that one thing at the peril of everything else in life. Mindfulness means that when giving time to something, be it a conversation, a meeting, answering emails, or playing with one's children, one is fully present with the activity at hand. Former President Bill Clinton to this day is well known for his ability to powerfully engage with people when meeting them. Individuals report that when in conversation with Clinton, "the world melts away and I have his full attention."

To give the gift of one's full attention, focus, and awareness may seem daunting. However, it is a skill anyone can learn. It starts by making a conscious choice that when saying hello to someone, all focus goes solely to that someone. And then when moving on to the next interaction, attention goes fully and solely to the next person.

As a leader, moving through a work day can seem something like Clinton's moving through a crowd of people who want his full attention. The leader's day may be filled with others' questions or concerns. It may not be until after 5:00 p.m. that the leader can start doing his or her actual "work." However, it is in these daily interactions where an immense amount of work occurs, and the quality of that work is proportional to the quality of the leader's attention during each interaction. Partial listening, quickly forgetting to-do's made in passing conversations, crafting emails while in conference calls, and texting during meetings are all habits that limit a leader's attentiveness and relational power.

Moment-to-moment mindfulness requires the kind of unfiltered focus on the person and situation at hand that we call "presence." This presence is a key element that shapes the quality of coaching a leader can provide. It influences the leader's ability to recognize coaching opportunities, and effects the way the coachee experiences his or her interaction with the leader.

In looking at our story about Chris, he showed mindfulness and presence as he moved deliberately toward his goal of bringing video gaming into Sun's business model. He had to rely on these tools as he climbed a seemingly impossible mountain. Each conversation mattered, each email mattered, and continuing to provide quality work mattered (why would a superior bother listening to an employee's ideas, if the employee is not seen as a high performer?). Chris exhibited the characteristics needed by every Coaching Leader in today's challenging business environment. Effective leaders must show up with mindfulness about limitless possibilities for themselves, for co-workers, and for their organizations.

Dog-Ear These Ideas

✓ *Focus fully on the task or interaction at hand. Let all other distractions melt away. Practice "burglar in the house" attentiveness: if woken in the middle of the night by a strange bang in the house, imagine the level of attention you would use figuring out what you just heard. Nothing else matters in that moment.*

✓ *Have a regular habit to practice and develop mindfulness – attention on the present moment. Examples include: exercise, meditation, reading, yoga, martial arts, gardening, and other creative hobbies.*

✓ *Use mindfulness to be "three level" mission driven. Your job and role exist to help the organization accomplish its mission (level 1). As a unique human being, your skills and interests exist to add unique value (level 2). And as a leader, your mission is to leave your organization in better stead than you found it (level 3).*

Conscious Listening

If a leader can take nothing else from this book, it is the hope that he or she will strive to be a better listener. The damage created by not listening well is enormous. Equally so are the benefits of high quality listening to the leader and followers in building shared trust, honesty, open communication, and improved performance.

Stealth coaching is at its most successful when the coach is deeply committed to listening. In fact, a majority of the coach's success will correlate directly to the quality of his or her listening. The deeper and more intent the listening, the more the coachee will be comfortable to share, reflect, and unearth his or her own solutions. Transformative coaching can oftentimes occur without the coach having to say very much. When the coach does speak from a foundation of listening and attentiveness, his or her comments have much more power, as they emerge from thoughtful insight, rather than from knee-jerk, impulsive, or rushed responses. Regardless of one's position, power, or experience, however, there are tough ramifications to poor listening. An example is outlined in the case below.

Ted, the director of a well-regarded non-profit organization, has a strong national reputation for his knowledge and track record of successful advocacy. Though his external partners, grantees, and funders appreciate his work ethic, contacts, and influence on a national stage, his staff struggles to follow him. They perceive him as arrogant, uncaring, and at times downright rude. The problem lies primarily in his lack of ability to listen. When employees enter his office, he is typically typing at his computer or is on the phone. He is busy working. But Ted fails to stop when people are present. When co-workers attempt to engage in conversation with him, he is often inattentive to their needs.

Brittany, a project lead and high performer on the team, describes her interactions with Ted this way: "When I go into his office, he rarely will look up from what he is doing. Or if he does look up, it's only briefly to say hello. It feels like he isn't interested in my situations, and I find myself having to repeat myself numerous times during the conversation. It makes me not want to talk anymore, and I certainly avoid dealing with him as much as possible. He makes me feel like I am a nuisance and a bother. I love the work we do, but I wish I could report to someone else."

Dennis, the deputy director, refers to Ted's style as "unintentional but damaging. He doesn't realize how everyone perceives him. I have tried talking to him about it, but he typically dismisses the critique by claiming he is simply busy. He says that multitasking is a common part of work now and that everyone should understand that. We've lost some really good people because they have grown tired of his neglect." The harder Ted works, cramming as much as he can into the workday, constantly doing two things at once, the more he isolates himself from his team.

One of the key areas in which leaders can always grow and develop is in their awareness skills. For most formal leaders, work days involve attending meetings and having people stop them (in the halls, in the office, in the bathroom) with questions. These recurring interactions are opportunities for leaders to notice and to make choices about how they want to interact. It is the compilation of these choices that create the leader's style and effectiveness.

The quality of the leader's attention, focus, and awareness in these many little moments shapes the leader's ability to gain and maintain willing followers. It also determines the leader's ability to foster employee self-motivation in owning and performing their work. It is the leader's job to pause amidst the chaos of the day and give his or her full focus and attention to the person seeking notice. Decisions are made in these small moments. Follower perceptions are developed through these engagements.

It is the leader's responsibility to be attentive to these moments while also balancing his or her own priorities. Is this an opportunity to coach? Is this a time to share technical knowledge? Is there enough time to dive into the issue, or does the leader need to clarify boundaries, setting a future time to meet? The leader's moment-to-moment awareness fuels the choices he or she makes throughout the day. Heightened attention helps clarify whether or not a coachable moment is presenting itself.

In coaching, listening is the fuel that drives the engine of inquiry. Peter Drucker, widely regarded as the father of modern management and a renowned expert on leadership, noted that "Listening (the first competency of leadership) is not a skill, it is a discipline. All you have to do is keep your mouth shut." Drucker also added that "The most important thing in communication is to hear what isn't being said." If Drucker is unequivocal in pointing out the vital importance of listening, why aren't leaders doing a better job of developing this skill? Perhaps the pressures brought on by unrelenting interruptions, the unspoken belief that they should have all the answers, and the expectation that they be available at all hours have combined to push leaders beyond their capabilities to listen effectively.

Danger, however, lies in failing to offer true listening. In an interaction between a leader and a follower, if the leader is demonstrating split attention – checking the phone, typing emails, or continually looking away – the follower knows that the leader is not fully present. This behavior has diminishing returns, as the follower can perceive from this lack of presence that the leader is uncaring, doesn't value others, or is perhaps untrustworthy. None of these outcomes may be the leader's intention, but perception is, of course, reality in the minds of followers.

Steven Covey, author of the popular book, *The Seven Habits of Highly Effective People*, said that, "Most people do not listen with the intent to understand; they listen with the intent to reply."[21] It is hard to be an effective leader when one comes from the ideology that providing output is more important than allowing input.

When the leader chooses to coach and starts truly listening, the coachee may not readily notice that a coaching conversation has begun. The coachee may, however, recognize that he or she has been given the stage to share thoughts, rationales, and unrevealed insights. The coachee has a positive experience, and there is no need for the leader to label it as coaching but rather to simply allow the space to exist.

Once the decision has been made to stealth coach, the quality of the coach's listening is a driving factor in the quality of the conversation. People generally employ three types of listening: in and out listening, hearing words, and empathetic listening.[22]

✓ *In and out listening* is noted by the listener paying attention in spurts, somewhat paying attention to the speaker but mostly focusing on themselves or their own tasks.

✓ *Hearing words listening* is the most deceptive of the three types, as it may appear that the listener is listening (eyes attentive to the listener, head nods, etc.), but the trick is that the listener makes little effort to understand the meaning of what is being said. Here, the listener may be listening for content, but he or she is missing the speaker's deeper meaning and emotional state.

✓ *Empathetic listening* includes the listener's awareness of the speaker's total communication. This includes listening not only for the speaker's content but also for the deeper meaning of what the speaker is experiencing.

Clearly empathetic listening is the most powerful type of the three. Here, the listener is focused on the present moment, not allowing his or her own judgments or thoughts to interfere with the ability to listen. The listener is placing him or herself in the speaker's position, aiming to see things from the speaker's point of view. A common phrase for this type of listening is to "stand in the other person's shoes." However, in order to stand in someone else's shoes, the listener has to first be willing to take off his or her own shoes. That is, the listener first sets aside his or her own beliefs, thoughts, judgments, and interpretations, before attempting to understand the speaker's unique perspective.

To summarize, in order to consciously listen, a leader who wants to coach needs to:

✓ Make a commitment to the value of listening as a core leadership competency, focusing his or her attention on the present moment,

✓ Set aside one's own judgments, and

✓ Seek to understand the coachee's situation, through curiosity and empathy.

Most of the cues and information needed to explore a situation with a coachee come from this conscious quality of listening. In fact, in most cases where quality coaching occurs, every good question or comment the coach makes comes from his or her listening. The coachee provides an endless amount of data for the coach. The coach simply needs to be present and open to seeing, hearing, and noticing all the cues.

Impatience, thinking more than listening, formulating the next question, and emotional responses are some of the many distractors that prevent the coach from fully participating as a conscious listener. Thus, the coach's brain is equally a great ally and a huge enemy in this process. How then, with so many distractions, does one be present in order to listen well for highly effective coaching?

It begins with attentiveness. When an athlete is performing at his or her best, he or she may be referred to as being highly attentive to the present moment, or "in the flow." In his 2008 updated classic, *Flow: The Psychology of Optimal Experience*, Dr. Mihaly Csikszentmihalyi describes this idea of presence as a state of consciousness, allowing for a deep and genuine enjoyment of life in the present moment.[23] Reaching this peak experience is attainable and certainly possible.

Here is a short practice to use anytime, as a way to transition from the last event to finding the present moment:

1. *Take a deep breath and feel the body's connection to the ground, pressure under the feet or against the floor...*

2. *Take a deep breath and notice any sounds in the present moment (birds chirping, machines humming, people talking)...*

3. *Take a deep breath and notice the activity of the mind thinking...*

4. *Imagine a chalk board in grade school. At the end of the day, after much use and erasing, the board has a visible film of chalk covering it. Visualize how it looks as it is wiped clean with a wet sponge; how clean, bright, and refreshed it looks. Now imagine doing the same sponge cleaning of the thoughts and mental "residue" that have built up across the mind.*

This may seem an awkward process at first. It feels unnatural and unfamiliar. Indeed it is, as the body and mind are being stretched to focus on the present moment rather than digesting the past or considering the future. What at first may take some time to adopt can soon become a quick refresher at any time throughout the day. This short practice pays huge dividends for both the leader's attentiveness to coach, as well as the impact it has on the coachee's experience and perception of the leader.

Dog-Ear These Ideas

✓ *When interrupted during a task, set boundaries and appropriate expectations. For example, if you are in a deadline-driven task or want to get your thoughts out to the email you are crafting, it is very appropriate to ask the interrupter for a moment to finish your thoughts or to come back at a specified time.*

✓ *When you stop an activity to engage with someone, turn away from distractors (computer screens, keyboards, phones, etc.), turn the down the volume of chatter in your head, and give your full focus, awareness, and attention to the speaker, even if only for a ten second conversation.*

✓ *Clarify how much time you have to talk when someone asks for some of your time. Be clear if you only have two minutes, but also be truthful if you have ten minutes, or even time to go get a cup of coffee or grab some lunch. Over-limiting others' access to you will ultimately impair your ability to be an effective leader and coach.*

✓ *Establish non-negotiable daily refreshers: mental, physical, emotional, or spiritual pauses from the turbulence of work. Wash the chalkboard.*

Driving the Coaching Conversation to Action: The Art and Science of Inquiry

As noted earlier, a fundamental principle of effective coaching is the coach's conviction that the coachee maintains the responsibility to resolve the issue at hand. The coach's focus is on the process of broadening the coachee's thinking, and driving the conversation towards action. Inquiry is the main vehicle for driving this type of strategic conversation.

The concept of inquiry can be found in numerous arenas, including science, education, development, and the arts. Inquiry can be framed and understood in numerous ways, though each with an eye on the learner's improvement and growth. At its essence inquiry involves:

✓ Gathering facts and making observations

✓ Exploring the world around us to foster curiosity of ourselves and our situations

✓ Asking questions with an interest towards revealing unseen possibilities

✓ Discovery – gaining new insights for understanding a situation or resolving a circumstance.

In each of the descriptors above there is a common distinction:

> *Inquiry expands one's ability to explore issues and to find possibilities and connections.*

In its application to coaching, the inquiry process can be viewed as helping coachees to discover new possibilities for thinking about a situation and choosing actions to get better results. In this context, "better" results could refer to more improved, measurable ways of handling a situation; more fulfilling outcomes to the person being coached; or results being more aligned with the organization's purpose.[24]

Going back to the situation between James and Kate (chapter 1, The Win-Win Power of Coaching), let us look at how James' use of inquiry and coaching moved Kate toward choosing actions to gain better results for herself and the organization. First, James helped Kate identify her main issue—that she was afraid to directly approach their boss, Pam, for the information she needed. Second, he provided support for Kate to reach out to Pam herself, by saying he would bring her along to his next meeting with Pam. Third, James helped Kate improve her own performance and that of the organization, when he offered to strategize with Kate as she prepared for her interaction with Pam. Additionally, Kate's dependency on James will decrease as she learns how to interact successfully with senior management.

The impact of these multiple positives far outweigh what might have been a routine interaction, with James taking Kate's "monkey" by getting the information she needs from Pam and bringing it back to her. The only real development in this non-coaching instance is that Kate gets to complete her project. But when James takes her monkey, Kate does not develop in terms of owning her own work, facing her fears, or developing strategies to get what she needs the next time she must interact with Pam.

The science of inquiry in a coaching context is to utilize questions to drive the coachee towards an implementable course of action. Though there are hundreds of coaching models, imbedded in almost all of them is a roadmap or process that moves the coachee from his or her present state to a preferred or desired state.

The stealth coaching process has three phases: clarifying, generating, and choosing. Each is explored through the posing of effective, non-judgmental, and powerful questions that are concise, open-ended, and that invite thinking.

Three major intentions support every coaching question:

1. to understand the coachee's situation from his or her perspective (clarifying questions)

2. to expand the coachee's thinking about his or her situation (possibilities questions)

3. to help the coachee move into action (commitments questions).

Questions have various purposes and varying impacts. There are essentially no bad questions, though the intent of a question may affect its value. And there are definitely better, more useful questions. If one reads through traditional coaching literature, one will find a litany of rules about questions: how to shape questions, what not to ask, types of questions to use or never to use. The list can be overwhelming and daunting enough to make any person who had interest in coaching want to give it up. Too many rules and restrictions shut down inquisitiveness, creativity, and willingness.

For stealth coaching, the focus is on "better" questions, ones that open possibility rather than limit, that expand thinking rather than close it off, and that are practical. Not all questions are or need to be powerful, awe-inspiring, or life changing. They simply are part of a larger line of inquiry.

The variety of questions used in coaching may include:

✓ Yes or no.

This is a simple question, but can be useful and important for clarification. For example, the coach may ask, "Do you work for Harold in the Contracting Office?" Since the coach here knows Harold, a yes answer helps the coach understand for the coachee's work environment.

Other examples of yes or no questions include:

- *Is Pam the only person who has the information you need?*

- *Is work-life balance a challenge for you?*

- *Would you go after a promotion if a job came available?*

- *Does the person you mention know he is challenging for you to work with?*

- *Can you imagine a scenario where things worked out exactly as you would hope?*

✓ Fact finding.

Specific information is vital to best understand the coachee's context, situation and perceptions. Many coaches falter by rushing through fact finding, moving to action too quickly. This type of question provides insight and clarity to both the coach and coachee. Examples of fact finding questions can vary from straight-forward to complex, such as "How long have you worked in Human Resources?" to "How much longer do you think you want to work in Human Resources?" Both of these are fact finding questions, yet they lend insight to the coachee's situation in completely different ways.

Other examples of fact finding questions include:

- *How important is it to you to get the answer you need from Pam?*

- *What would good work-life balance look like to you?*

- *What is the next ideal job for you and what are its components?*

- *What about this person makes it challenging for you?*

- *What is missing for you from getting the exact outcome you would like?*

✓ Tapering or narrowing.

A common coaching occurrence is that the coachee identifies multiple issues or possibilities to explore. Coaches and/or coachees rarely have endless time to thoroughly explore all the raised options in one conversation. Therefore, a strategy the coach can use is to narrow the conversation utilizing a well-crafted question. For example, the coach might say, "It sounds like we have identified four different strategies you could take. Given that we only have about five more minutes to talk this morning, which one would you like to focus on today?" or, "I have to leave for my next meeting in seven minutes. What would be the best use of our time? What would you most like to focus on now?" In each instance, the coach is inviting the coachee to narrow the conversation to a specific topic or item. The power in this line of inquiry is that it allows the coachee to make the decision, giving him or her stronger empowerment and ownership of the conversation.

Further examples of tapering or narrowing questions include:

- *Which of these strategies seems like the most useful for you to get access to Pam?*

- *Of the work-life balance components we have been discussing, which part is most critical that we discuss now?*

- *Of all the characteristics of your ideal job, which is most imperative?*

- *Which strategy for dealing with this person would you like to explore first?*

- *In getting your preferred outcome, what step are you willing to take immediately?*

✓ Advice Giving.

Wanting to offer advice is the stickiest trap for many coaches early in their development. A major temptation for the coach, often driven by a habit and reinforced by its efficiency, is to provide answers, opinions, and solutions. These are wonderful attributes to foster, except when utilizing the mindset and skills of coaching, as they sabotage the coaching conversation, leaving the coachee without having to think for him or herself. As the coach listens to the coachee, ideas, suggestions, and solutions will typically flood the coach's mind. Rather than maintaining the coaching mindset – that the coachee has the ability to solve his or her own problem – the coach may give advice masked in the form of a question. This may sound like, "Have you considered joining Toastmasters? Because I've heard they are a great organization for improving presentation skills." Or, "You know, would it be smart to look through the policy files before you take action on this?" Or, "Isn't it best you just start looking for a new job, rather than continue to deal with your nasty boss?"

> *When the coach gives opinions it undermines the conversation, disempowering the coachee's ownership, self-accountability, and problem resolution.*

Other examples of what <u>not</u> to say, as they have the coach's advisement embedded in them:

- *Did you know Pam always takes lunch late, around 1:30, which would be a great time to show up at her office?*

- *Have you thought about asking your boss for more flexibility on Fridays, like working four longer days so you can leave early on Fridays?*

- *Isn't your ideal job something you'll have to leave this company to get?*

- *Do you know about the mediation services provided by Human Resources?*

- *If you don't get your ideal outcome, might you consider filing a grievance?*

✓ Powerful questions.

When the coach asks a question that causes the coachee to pause, to slow down, to reflect, or even to verbalize "that is a good question," the coach is most likely tapping into the realm of powerful questioning. This type of inquiry encourages the coachee to enter a deeper level of thinking, perhaps expanding, reframing, or challenging the coachee's current thought processes, perceptions, or beliefs. An example of a powerful question could be, "What is the most pressing concern for you in regard to this issue?" or, "What assumptions are you making about this scenario that we may be overlooking?"

Other examples of powerful questions include:

- *What is the one thing you would change about this situation to get the information you need in a more timely fashion?*

- *What does an ideal balance of work and home life look like to you?*

- *Imagine you could acquire your ideal job today; what would you be doing and where?*

- *If you had the power to make this person behave however you wanted, what would you want to change about him?*

- *If you had magic pixie dust and could sprinkle it on this situation, enabling you to get the exact outcome you wanted, what would that be?*

There are multiple types of inquiry. Each is relevant and practical to use. Yet with all of the examples above, there is no guarantee that if the coach asks these or any other scripted questions, the coachee will open up more, shift perspective, or be moved to a deeper level of thinking and strategizing. Each coachee is different and will respond uniquely to questions based upon many conditions. Common issues affecting the effectiveness of any line of inquiry include:

✓ The coachee's topic.

- The situation brought forth by the coachee may or may not be one that invites stealth coaching. A simple assessment is to gauge whether the coachee's issue involves a known, clear, and correct solution. Such issues do not invite stealth coaching, as they do not involve several options for action. Topics for which there could be a variety of approaches fitting the coachee's needs are ones suitable for stealth coaching.

✓ The coachee's readiness.

- The coach may or may not be able to gauge this at first. Questions the coach can consider in the first few moments of an interaction include: Does the coachee seem open and willing to engage with the topic? What is the coachee's emotional and mental state? What is the coachee's overall enthusiasm to be coached? If verbal and non-verbal coachee cues indicate that the current moment is not the time to explore coaching, the coach can offer to schedule a time to talk or otherwise be available to the coachee when he or she is ready.

✓ The timing and/or location.

- Given the nature of the issue, the coachee may not respond well if the conversation happens in a public venue versus a private one. Additionally, the coach or coachee may not be mentally or emotionally ready to tackle the issue, depending on when it is raised and the state that either person is in at that moment. Shifting the location or scheduling a time to converse can positively affect either party.

✓ Diversity or cultural context.

- Is the issue being raised one that the coach can proficiently handle? This is a tricky topic for many, as it involves the coach assessing his or her own blind spots or cultural insensitivities. For example, there may not be a coach/coachee match if racial, socioeconomic, or national differences are not able to be comfortably bridged. Language, physical, or behavioral expectations may not be in sync. A sensitive coach can identify if he or she is the best fit to help the coachee. This is not an invitation for the coach to escape attempting to coach, nor is it an excuse to disengage from others. Rather it is an opportunity for the coach to explore the biases and limitations within him or herself.

✓ The way questions are asked.

- This speaks to the artfulness of coaching, vital especially when stealth coaching. Vocal tone, wording, and nonverbal cues all influence how the coachee receives questions. Tone and nonverbal can impact or be affected by the diversity and cultural issues noted above. For example, the simple question of "How could you possibly handle that?" can be perceived in very different ways based on how it is delivered. If stated with the following word stressed: "how could you possibly *handle* that?" the coachee is invited to consider possibilities for dealing with the situation. On the contrary, if stated as: "How could *you... possibly* handle *that?*" the question can sound unsupportive and threatening, as if the coach believes the coachee is incapable of effectively dealing with the situation.

✓ The coach's readiness.

- There are numerous factors that can impede the coach's ability, such as indifference to being an authority, fear of conflict, confidence as a coach, or history between the coach and coachee. Timing, context, and topic, as described in this section, can impact the coach's readiness as well.

Dog-Ear These Ideas

✓ *When coaching, always keep the bigger picture in mind: that the intention of the coaching conversation is to move the coachee towards discovery and action.*

✓ *Train yourself to ask questions first, in any situation, rather than to give away answers.*

✓ *Practice noticing the mental and emotional states of others. Look for nonverbal clues such as facial expressions and body language. Listen for vocal tone and choice of words as indicators. Take in others' overall "vibe," the energy or message they project. For example, a teenager with green hair, torn clothes, and lots of piercings is sending a strong message to the world of how he wants to be perceived. Or at work, notice when a colleague is visibly troubled by her display of folded arms, a furrowed brow, and lowered gaze.*

✓ *Recognize that solid questions come from good listening. The appropriate next good question comes from staying present, in the moment, with the coachee.*

✓ *Understand that it is an easy trap for a coach to rush the coachee quickly to solutions rather than to clarify the situation fully or to explore various options and possibilities.*

✓ *Watch detective shows or read mystery novels. As the story unfolds, imagine asking the characters different types of questions (from "yes and no" to "powerful questions") to hone your skills for inquiry.*

SECTION III

IMPLEMENTATION

First Steps: The Assessment of Readiness

Applying coaching skills can initially be very tricky. Employees and colleagues can be quite astute to a person's change in typical ways of interacting with them. Thus the theme of this book: to be stealthful when coaching.

How does a leader first start to implement stealth coaching skills and strategies? Here are three simple questions to use as a road map towards coaching:

1) *Is this topic or situation a coachable opportunity?*

   If the coach's instinct is to give an answer or resolve an issue, those are good indicators to explore the possibility of coaching rather than problem solving.

2) *Is this a coachable moment? Is the time, place, and setting appropriate?*

   If not, can adjustments be made to support coaching? For example, take a hallway conversation back to a private office or meeting space.

3) *Is the coachee in a mindset to be coached? If not, can a time to talk be scheduled for the near future?*

   If the coachee appears overwhelmed emotionally, "brain fried" from a long day, or highly stressed and unable to process at the time, give the person some time to recompose themselves before coaching him or her.

If the situation presents itself or a time has been set aside when coaching can occur, then how does the leader introduce coaching stealthfully? The first step is to establish the groundwork that the leader is going to begin the conversation by asking some questions. Here are a few phrases to try:

✓ *Sounds like a lot. I want to make sure I have all the facts correct in my mind. Do you mind if I ask you a few questions to get some clarity on the issue?*

✓ *Given the problem you have described, what have you tried so far, or do you have any ideas that you could try?*

✓ *This is a complex issue; perhaps we should take a walk and get some coffee so I can hear more. Do you have 10 minutes to go to the cafeteria together?*

✓ *How can I support you in taking on this challenge?*

✓ *This is a thought-provoking situation. Why don't we sit down and think this through together.*

✓ *If you had to resolve this issue on your own, what might you do?*

These are all examples of how to gently transform a conversation from one where the leader is giving answers to one where the field is open to a dialogue. Once the leader has established this framework, it becomes much easier and less threatening to ask a few questions, perhaps opening the conversation to a deeper line of inquiry and exploration. What appears as a basic question is actually the beginning of a coaching relationship.

Another strategy is to always start by asking one or two clarifying questions and then default back to the typical strategy of giving solutions or input. This is not an overt or threatening strategy but rather a gentle way to introduce inquiry into conversations. Over time, start with three or four questions before defaulting back. Eventually start with five or six questions. Gradually introduce and change the methodology to one of coaching to make the interactions more "normal" to the coachee.

Last, a common strategy leaders use to push others towards self-referral is to require the bringing of solutions with problems. Creating the expectation that an employee will generate at least one possible solution to a problem he or she brings the leader begins the process of the coachee broadening his or thinking before the conversation has even begun. Clear expectations of personal accountability such as this can crack the coaching door open before the engagement has begun. Coachee-generated ideas and solutions beg for clarity and inquiry, the beginning of a stealth coaching conversation.

Dog-Ear These Ideas

- ✓ *Follow the T.M.M. approach to assess a coaching opportunity: Topic, Moment, Mindset. Is the topic coachable? Is the timing right? Is the coachee in a good state of mind to be coached?*

- ✓ *Develop opening lines that invite stealth coaching. Examples are provided above. Use these or modify them to suit your own language and needs.*

- ✓ *Set expectations for yourself and those around you. Make it a norm that you routinely ask questions and seek clarity.*

- ✓ *With employees, make it clear that problems they present to you should also be accompanied with at least one idea for a solution.*

Introducing and Unveiling Stealth Coaching in the Workplace

There are many ways to move workplace conversations toward a coaching format. What can differ dramatically is *how* the coaching emerges in the conversation. Explicit and subtle coaching are two very different strategies, the latter referring to stealth coaching. For coaching to be effective in the workplace, especially at first, the leader can allow it to slide gently into the conversation.

For example, an employee enters the manager's office, looking for help for an issue he has. The manager's typical style is to ask the employee what the problem is and quickly jump to providing solutions or actions steps. Since coaching involves listening and inquiry, moving the conversation in that direction could seem unusual and awkward to both the manager and the employee. Instead, the manager could say one of the following:

✓ *Why don't we sit down and think this through together?*

✓ *How about if we grab a cup of coffee and talk about it?*

✓ *This sounds complicated. Help me understand where things stand now.*

Each of these statements opens the door for the manager to ask some clarifying questions. There should be nothing unusual about the manager, the leader, or the decision maker trying to understand the situation a bit better before giving her or his opinion. A coachee's resistance can emerge as the coach continues on a line of inquiry rather than jumping to providing a solution. This is a critical moment in the conversation. If met with resistance by the coachee, the manager/coach could say one of the following:

✓ *This is a critical issue, and I don't want to jump to a solution too quickly. Tell me a bit more. What have you thought of as ideas of what to do?*

✓ *I'm not certain yet what I would suggest. Can you tell me where things stand now? If you could do anything, what would you do?*

✓ *You are on the ground level with this situation and have been dealing with it well so far. I have ideas, and I would like to hear yours, as well.*

A coaching conversation might break down, even to the point where the coachee calls out the coach. For example, the coachee might say, "Why do you keep asking me questions? Just tell me what I am supposed to do!" Or, "What's going on here? I am not used to you asking me so many questions." Or, "Look, I am just not sure what to do!" The coaching framework is not like other conversations, and the coachee may find it uncomfortable. He or she may not be used to having the space to think, to be challenged to problem solve, or to be held accountable to make a decision. Coaching can move people out of their comfort zones. What can the coach say at this point? Here are a few strategies:

✓ *I hear you are frustrated. My concern is that if I just give you my answer, you won't have learned how to problem solve for yourself. I want to see you grow as a leader, and I believe you can handle this one.*

✓ *You're right: I am asking you a lot of questions. This is a complex situation and I want to make sure we have the entire picture clear. You have described the situation, and I want to see what your perspective is on possible solutions, since you are the one who has to handle this issue.*

✓ *Ok, I know, this is weird and different. I am trying a different strategy with you because I know you have the capacity to resolve this situation. If I just give you my opinion on what to do, I am limiting your abilities to be a leader.*

These answers, especially the last one, push the boundary of unveiling that coaching is occurring. However, until the coach labels the conversation as "coaching," it remains only a novel dialogue style. Once the coach calls out that she or he is trying to coach, the coachee gains clearer footing to identify the strategy in the future. This may not be a problem, but the word "coaching" may come with negative connotations. If the coachee finally asks, "Is this coaching?" there is no need to deny. Be truthful and transparent, still with an eye towards the coachee's development. Try one of these:

✓ *Yes, I have been trying to coach. I have found it useful myself to develop my leadership skill, and I think it could be effective for you, too. Would you like to try it a little longer and see where it takes us? If it doesn't seem helpful, we can drop it.*

✓ *Yes, it is. I have been micromanaging too much, always telling you what to do. I have recently been reminded that I didn't grow until I had mentors and managers who gave me the space to learn and grow. So I wanted to give you the same opportunity.*

✓ *I know you want me to tell you what to do. Here's the thing: if I give you my opinion, you tend to believe that's the only way to do it. I want you to learn to be more creative and to trust your own ideas. And I want to be clear that it is okay if you try your own solutions, and if it doesn't go well, it is okay by me. It's okay to make mistakes. It's part of how you grow as a professional and as a leader.*

Though the guidelines outlined in this book provide a structure for navigating successful coaching interactions, everyone is different, and there is no one right way to be a stealth coach. The better the coach knows her or his coachees, the better the coach can adapt to each coachee's style. Additionally, the better the coach knows her or himself, understands her or his strengths and weaknesses as a coach and as a communicator, the better the coach can manage her or his interactions and strategies to introduce coaching.

Dog-Ear These Ideas

✓ *Seek opportunities to invite coaching into the conversation.*

✓ *Find the language that works for you to get the stealth coaching ball rolling.*

✓ *Recognize when the coachee is becoming reluctant or resistant, and have a backup plan.*

✓ *When the coaching is not getting traction with the coachee, be transparent by labeling your strategy and why you chose to try it with him or her.*

✓ *Get to know the people you want to coach. Rapport, trust, honesty, and respect are at the heart of effective coaching.*

When to Stealth Coach

There are countless opportunities to utilize coaching skills in the workplace, because there are innumerable interactions between human beings in the workplace. Not every interaction is a coaching opportunity, however. The coach's challenge is to assess opportunities in the moment, situations that up until now may have presented themselves through other types of conversations. Here are a few examples:

1. An employee had a poor interaction with a customer on the phone. This was the third such impropriety by the employee this month.

    A typical response: Provide corrective feedback or even punish the employee.

2. A colleague is having a conflict with one of her direct reports. They don't like each other but must work together. The colleague realizes she has been avoiding doing anything about this and that it's time for a discussion with the direct report, but she doesn't feel she knows where to begin. She asks for guidance.

    A typical response: Advise the colleague with solutions and strategies to fix the problem.

3. A direct report feels he is ready for a promotion. He is a decent performer but is clearly not prepared for advancement just yet. However, he is persistent and has begun to voice public dissatisfaction with management and the organization. The quality of his work has begun to slide as well.

    A typical response: Temper the employee's behavior through direct conversations, or avoid it and hope he leaves.

4. A teammate lacks life balance. She keeps long hours, feels burned out, and often has little resilience. She wants to improve her quality of life but doesn't know how. As a trusted peer, she seeks your advice on what to do.

    A typical response: Sympathize with the teammate, having not found any great solutions for your own overwork and stress.

In workplace situations like those above, it is easy to give knee-jerk responses based on the leader's own experience with the topic, impressions about the issue, or feelings towards the person. However, each of the examples above is a potential coaching situation. When the leader looks through the lens of helping others help themselves, the possibility for coaching emerges:

1. An employee had a poor interaction with a customer on the phone. This was the third such impropriety by the employee this month.

    A stealth coaching response: I've noticed this isn't the first tough interaction you have had with a customer lately. What do you see going on in these situations?

2. A colleague is having a conflict with one of her direct reports. They don't like each other but must work together. The colleague realizes she has been avoiding doing anything about this and that it's time for a discussion with the direct report, but doesn't feel like she knows where to begin. She asks for guidance.

A stealth coaching response: What would a successful conversation with your direct report look like? How would it go?

3. A direct report feels he is ready for a promotion. He is a decent performer but is clearly not ready for advancement just yet. However, he is persistent and has begun to voice public dissatisfaction with management and the organization. The quality of his work has begun to slide as well.

A stealth coaching response: I understand your frustration with not getting promoted as quickly as you would like. Given the nature of the job you seek, what do you see as your strengths and weaknesses in performing in that role today?

4. A teammate lacks life balance. She keeps long hours, feels burned out, and often has little resilience. She wants to improve her quality of life but doesn't know how. As a trusted peer, she seeks your advice on what to do.

A stealth coaching response: What is quality life balance to you?

These examples of alternative responses to employee situations illustrate how quickly and easily one can overlook coaching opportunities (and the simplicity in which conversations can be transformed towards coaching). Providing quick or habitual solutions happens every day, and that approach is not always negative. It is part of the culture of work for leaders to have solutions and provide direction. For stealth coaching to take place, though, this impulse needs to be quelled just enough for the recognition that other possibilities may be available.

In making this change, the leader may begin to see many opportunities to stealth coach, such as when he or she:

✓ Conducts an exit interview

✓ Assigns tasks or projects

✓ Offers career counseling and employee development strategies

✓ Gives feedback

✓ Helps others develop skills and abilities

✓ Helps others overcome setbacks or challenges

✓ Brings new employees on board with an orientation

✓ Handles performance appraisals

✓ Deals with an employee having a performance problem

✓ Engages an employee who has failed to do something "right"

✓ Responds to an employee who wants help or guidance

✓ Encounters someone who needs a sounding board or wants to vent

✓ Faces those who want to give their monkeys away.

These are a few of the many opportunities for which coaching can be a useful tool. As leaders develop their awareness to use coaching, more and more opportunities will become evident. The question is not *when* or *how*; rather, it is *if* to stealth coach. The coach's mindset is to have a bias to lean towards listening and inquiry as a stealthful way to both investigate and determine if it may be an appropriate time to coach.

Dog-Ear These Ideas

✓ *As a way to train yourself to notice coaching opportunities, after an interaction ask yourself, "Was there an opportunity to coach in that conversation?"*

✓ *Ask at least one question at the start of any discussion. It may effortlessly start a stealth coaching conversation.*

✓ *Notice just how many possibilities exist to coach in the workplace. Reference the list above for ideas, and attune your awareness to others as you move through your day.*

Who to Stealth Coach First

A common trap for leaders and managers is to try out new skills and strategies on their most challenging employees, those individuals who are lower performing or who have difficult personalities. The problem with this approach is that typically the nature of that relationship has limits and barriers. There may not be a high enough level of trust, respect, or rapport (among other issues) between the manager and the employee. If the manager tries a new tool with these challenging workers, the employee is apt to resist, deflect, fight against, or even ignore the manager's attempts to engage.

Coaching is no different. The basic human response is often to drop coaching as an option because it "did not work." The person attempting to coach is frustrated. The coachee is frustrated. And the tool gets dropped from the leader's toolbox for good, as experience has proven that it does not work.

To have a successful interaction and reinforce the use of coaching, the coach needs to first engage with higher (but not the highest) performers. In considering the range of employee engagement, at the highest end there are those who are simply self-disposed to deliver high quality work. These individuals are a rare and valuable find; they can be placed into almost any workplace and will find a way to succeed. It is a natural part of their makeup. This population typically requires less support to foster and achieve success. They may not be as hungry for coaching since they already demonstrate high acuity in critical thinking, problem solving, decision making, leading, and the like.

It is the next level of employees who are most ripe for coaching. These people are hungry, eager, excited and want to grow. They actively seek professional development and may have lots of ideas and passion to do quality work. What they lack are some or many of the skills seen in the self-disposed population. They are open to feedback and want to develop themselves as leaders. These people are the ones with whom to start stealth coaching.

Finding success early will encourage the coach to continue using these skills, to hone the process further, and to make it a more regularly used tool. A receptive coachee will be more forgiving of the coach's early lack of mastery. With an appropriate match, the coach will not get as easily discouraged and the coachee will remain available, while both learn and grow in the coaching process.

Dog-Ear These Ideas

✓ Do not practice your coaching skills on your lower performers at first. They will not be receptive and you will become easily frustrated. As Mark Twain said, "Never try to teach a pig to sing. It wastes time and annoys the pig."

✓ Do practice your coaching with your eager and excited employees. They are much more apt to be open and receptive to your coaching approach.

✓ Coach others for both performance issues and for their development and growth.

✓ Make a firm commitment to coach at least once a week. Be intentional in trying out various coaching skills or components. One week it may be to improve your listening. The next week it could be to enhance the quality of questions. The following week it is to move the conversation towards action. Stay focused on increasing your skills and confidence in all aspects of coaching.

Stealth Coaching With Peers

Coaching peers, the stakes tend to be lower than when coaching employees or superiors. There are no reporting issues, which removes power dynamics and perceived oppression. Collegial coaching can typically be a bit more transparent. Given the level of trust and rapport, the coach may even give open invitations, such as:

✓ *Sounds interesting. Do you want to brainstorm ideas of what to do?*

✓ *We could grab some coffee and talk about how you could handle this. How's that sound?*

✓ *How can I help? Want to talk it through? Perhaps a little bit of coaching? Or do you want me to just listen?*

Meredith, a highly skilled IT manager in a small but fast growing company, is struggling to meet one of her client's needs. The client's requests and scope of work seem to change daily. Meredith has grown frustrated after a month of trying to pin the client down for more specifics. Finally, on the way to the cafeteria one day, she crosses paths with Jeff:

Jeff: Hi Meredith. How's it going? Haven't seen you in a while.

Meredith: Yeah, I'm okay, I suppose. Actually, sorry, you caught me at a weird time.

Jeff: How so?

Meredith: You know that client project I've been assigned to?

Jeff: Oh, the new client downtown?

Meredith: Yeah, that one. Well, I've been working with their point person, Janice, for a month now, and I can't seem to get

---

clear on what she wants. It seems like every time I ask for clarity, she changes the scope of everything that is needed.

Jeff: Wow, that stinks. They are a big client for us, too. Are you grabbing a bite to eat? Do you have time to sit and chat about it? Don't know if I can be of help, but I can try.

Meredith: Actually, that would be great. My boss is always so busy; I can't get time with him to talk about what to do.

Jeff: Are you okay if I ask you questions to better understand the whole situation? Then we can figure out what you could do. Kind of a mini coaching talk? How's that sound?

Meredith: Great. I also want to make sure whatever we come up with will be okay with my boss. Let me grab my food and then we can get started.

Jeff: Alright, see you in a second.

In this situation, Meredith is able to identify her issue and to see how her peer, Jeff, can be of help. Jeff recognizes this encounter as an opportunity to stealth coach. If Meredith was overwhelmed or otherwise resistant to talking, moving into stealth coaching may not be an appropriate strategy to try. In this case, there is less at stake for Jeff to try it. If worse comes to worst, Jeff or Meredith may identify that coaching is not the support she needs at that moment.

Dog-Ear These Ideas

✓ *Be more transparent on your desire to coach your colleagues. The worst they can say is "no thank you."*

✓ *Ask a trusted peer if you can practice your coaching with him or her. It is a safer relationship in which to work on your skills.*

✓ *Share your knowledge of coaching with him or her. Share a copy of this book to begin a dialogue about coaching.*

✓ *Form a reading group to explore stealth coaching together.*

Stealth Coaching With Superiors

As leaders learn coaching skills and methods, they commonly ask: "Can you coach up...can you coach your boss?" This is not an easy question. Several elements must be in place for the opportunity to coach up the organizational chart, including these:

✓ Trust   This is the foundation for almost any relationship and is the main basis by which a superior will allow for coaching from a direct report.

✓ Rapport   Rapport is a byproduct of trust (though not mutually exclusive). There needs to be a decent relationship between the direct report and superior. If they do not like each other, coaching won't work or even be an option.

✓ Respect   If the superior does not see the direct report as credible, as high performing, or as a knowledgeable resource, why would he or she possibly be open to the direct report's coaching? Conversely, if the direct report does not respect the superior, then coaching may be phony or manipulative.

✓ Time   Is the superior available? Does time exist on his or her calendar to engage in a coaching conversation?

The simplest way to stealthfully introduce and engage in coaching a superior is to remain in the mode of seeking clarity. For example:

✓ *I'm not sure I understand everything you need from our team for this project. Can you tell me a bit more?*

✓ *If this strategy went perfectly, how would you see me and my team playing a role?*

✓ *Is there any chance of this not going as planned? Are there any assumptions we may be making?*

✓ *Before our next meeting, what would you like to see accomplished?*

As the superior gets more comfortable being asked clarifying questions, the direct report may use inquiry geared towards different ideas and approaches, expanding the superior's thinking:

✓ *So given the situation, I can think of a couple additional ideas we could try. Would you like to hear them? Do you have any other ideas, as well?*

✓ *I wonder what could happen if we try that strategy. Can we talk about pros and cons?*

✓ *I don't know if this is going to play out as we think. What are some limiting factors that we haven't discussed?*

✓ *Aside from our challenges, this also seems like a great opportunity. If you could have this situation turn out exactly as you wanted, what would that look like?*

To coaching superiors, one must be highly astute and nimble. The coach needs to closely attend to the superior's responsiveness, monitoring when to ease off and when to explore further. Coaching does not appear threatening when wording is sensitively chosen. Taking a stance of needing clarity allows for inquiry to be appropriate. "We" and "us" statements make inquiry sound more collaborative. Discussing impact and outcomes moves the conversation away from "you and me" and onto an outside topic a leader and superior can handle together.

Another key issue of coaching, mentioned above, is timing. Is the superior rushed? Is there time to talk? Is there an openness to brainstorm? Is the superior more open when talking in his or her office, in the direct report's office, out of the office, at lunch, or taking a short walk? Finding the right time and place can greatly impact the quality and likelihood of coaching to emerge with a superior.

Political savvy also informs one's ability to coach up. The direct report needs to have a good understanding of the world in which the superior works. It is a common occurrence for a direct report to blame a superior for what is not working at his or her level or in the organization as a whole. If the direct report can have an understanding of the pressures and politics affecting the superior's thinking and decision-making philosophy, the direct report can better tailor a line of inquiry that makes sense to the superior. For example:

- ✓ *I don't understand why you want us to do it that way,* is less tactful than, *I can see why you would want us to go about it that way. I think I have an idea that would actually make it more efficient and produce better results for you and the organization. Would you be willing to look at additional possibilities?*

- ✓ *Whatever you say,* is less helpful than, *this is a good strategy. In looking at its implementation, where do you see potential limitations or stressors to our resources?*

- ✓ *You don't seem to listen to anyone else's ideas,* is more confrontational than, *I don't know if this will work out as you think. Can we discuss the impact of this option?*

Going back to the example in the previous chapter, Jeff has done some coaching with his colleague, Meredith, about her situation dealing with a tricky client. It is a major contract for their company, and they both understand the critical nature of how she handles these interactions. From their peer coaching time, the idea Meredith created and likes best is to ask the client to partner with her to shape a six-month project plan before they proceed any further in their work together. This is a slightly radical notion, given how their company has typically engaged with clients in the past. Meredith is concerned her boss, Carey, may not approve, and Meredith and Jeff prepare Meredith for her conversation with Carey. She has her weekly one-on-one meeting with Carey the next day.

Carey: So where do things stand with Janice and our new project?

Meredith: I wanted to talk to you about that. It's been a little tricky so far.

Carey: What's going on?

Meredith: The factors outlined in the original contract are not what Janice seems to want now. She changes her mind almost daily, and it has been tough to have a consistent idea of what we should be implementing for them.

Carey: That's normal, Meredith; you know that, especially with a new client and something of this complexity.

Meredith: Of course, and I am also recognizing that her requests are creeping outside the scope of the contract.

Carey: Well, we can't lose this contract; it's a big one for us. Just please keep her happy.

Meredith: Of course.

Carey: I need you to stay focused on giving her what she needs. That is your first priority.

Meredith: Can I ask you a question? How do you handle working with people who change their minds frequently?

Carey: That's my life every day. Between the board of directors, our legal team, and requests from the CEO and CFO, I am always changing directions.

Meredith: Doesn't that get frustrating?

Carey: Some days it does. What I have come to learn is that change is constant, and I have to be prepared to go with the flow. That's what is happening for you with Janice.

Meredith: When you and your husband were having your new house built, and the timelines were getting pushed back so much by the contractor, can you remind me what you did to get it back on track?

Carey: That was a mess! Sure, my husband and I met with the contractor to reinforce our desires and got involved in creating a plan together for what would happen. That was much better than just sitting back waiting for updates from him.

Meredith: And did that help?

Carey: Oh, substantially. It wasn't perfect, but it was much, much better.

Meredith: So if you imagine Janice is in the same boat you and your husband were. I, as her "contractor" am not able to stay on the timelines she first asked for, because she wants to change where the stove will go in the kitchen, or how many recessed lights will be in the living room. I would like to sit down with her, much like you did with your contractor, and lay out a project plan together. Every time I try to do it alone, to meet her changing requests, it pushes things back and she gets frustrated. If she and I create a plan together, could we have similar success that you did with your contractor?

Carey: That's an interesting way to describe it. Okay, I see where things stand more clearly now. Sure, let's try your idea. Do you need me in that meeting?

Meredith: I think what would be most useful is if you contacted Janice to make the suggestion, as if it were yours. I think having it come from your mouth will be much more persuasive than having it come from me. If she is receptive, I am comfortable meeting with her alone.

Carey: Sounds good. I will call her later this morning.

Meredith: Thank you, Carey. I appreciate your support and help.

Superiors are generally coachable. If the proper foundations are in place and the direct report skillfully employs courage, willingness, and good timing, the relationship between direct report and superior can be transformed. The coach needs to develop a keen eye and ear for coachable moments, and also have the astuteness to recognize when to back off.

Dog-Ear These Ideas

✓ *Recognize how credible your superiors consider you to be. The higher the credibility, the more possibility to coach them.*

✓ *Test the waters of stealth coaching a superior by asking only a single clarifying question. Notice how he or she responds to that simple inquiry.*

✓ *If you have employees reporting to you, be open to their coaching. Your responsiveness will give you a better sense of strategies to try with your superiors.*

✓ *Don't assume that coaching up will always be possible. Pick your opportunities selectively.*

SECTION IV

BARRIERS AND CHALLENGES

The Leader's Dilemma: Challenges in the Information and Multitasking Age

Monica, a senior manager in a large university hospital, describes her work life as "being propelled a hundred miles an hour while juggling twelve balls, helping employees and customers, and staying up to date on the latest trends in technology." She struggles to find free time on her calendar, which gets constantly filled with employee needs, weekly meetings, project deadlines, demands from the CFO, and customer requests. Some days she forgets to eat lunch, and she even struggles to find five minutes to go to the restroom! Monica is very good at her job, but she has no time to appreciate it, due to the constant barrage of communication, emails, interruptions, expectations, deadlines and emergencies. Her employees know she is busy, but struggle to have enough access to her to get the answers and guidance they need.

Like Monica, we are burdened. For many of us, the standard nine-to-five work day is a thing of the past. Our brains are overloaded with information and demands both at work and at home, and we try to make sense of it all as quickly as possible, integrating new data with already known information. Yet when driven to distraction by multitasking, by accessing information at any time, or by answering emails on our phones at 11:00 at night, we are creating an imbalance.

In this age of knowledge-based workers and apparent endless information streams, rapid growth, transformation of technological advances, and pressures to keep up with work demands, the strain to be effective tightens. It has become socially acceptable to be in meetings and use our phones to check email or access the web. It is seemingly allowable to have a hallway conversation with someone while they are texting. We are squeezed with multitasking and information processing and our brains are trying to keep up! There is more information in a week's worth of *New York Times* newspapers than average people living in the 1800's would have had encountered in their entire lives.[25] No wonder we are experiencing overload and are less than fully attentive to our colleagues.

Colliding with this overloaded work style is the human relationship of leaders and followers. Building rapport, communicating expectations, making decisions, clarifying roles and responsibilities, creating a culture of buy-in and success, maximizing talent and bringing out the best in ourselves and others – these are leadership skills and expectations. None of these can be well accomplished without reflection, without pausing amid daily chaos to find some clarity before taking the next action. It is in these moments of reflection that a leader can identify options and choose new strategies: listening versus talking, considering versus doing, reflecting versus reflexively responding, or coaching versus directing. Successful leaders need to create space for themselves and their colleagues to step away from the electronic information stream.

Dog-Ear These Ideas

✓ *Realize that when dealing with people, multitasking is a challenge to effective leadership.*

✓ *Set down the phone or electronic gizmo when engaged in conversation.*

✓ *Have established "no electronics" times every day at home.*

✓ *At the start of meetings, have everyone stack their cell phones in the middle of the table.*

✓ *Take a short mental break at least once or twice a day.*

Overcoming Predictable Barriers and Challenges

Being a stealth coach is not as easy as buying pizzas at lunch and having people come running to visit. Employees, colleagues and bosses will most likely not come running for coaching. In fact, they may look at the coach like he or she has two heads at first, especially if the coach pushes these new tools too hard or too quickly. Patience, persistence, and a focus on the big picture will all help keep the coach in the appropriate mindset to continually seek and find coaching opportunities.

Predictable challenges to coaching are:

✓ Resistance to coaching

✓ Finding time for coaching

✓ Temptation to manage versus coach.

As introduced in chapter 14 (Introducing and Unveiling Stealth Coaching in the Workplace), a common barrier to coaching is coachee resistance. The coachee may respond in a number of ways that indicate he or she does not want to engage in a coaching conversation, such as:

✓ *Why aren't you interrupting me by now? Usually you have an idea already.*

✓ *I feel like I am doing all the talking. Don't you have anything to add?*

✓ *Why are you asking me so many questions?*

✓ *Will you please just tell me what to do!*

In these examples, the coachee is not used to being heard so attentively or being asked for insights and opinions. This can certainly be uncomfortable at first for anyone. The coach needs to start slowly. Do not "jump into the deep end of the pool" and become a leader who only asks questions and never provides input or solutions. This is a recipe for disaster and potential political suicide in the workplace. When first introducing a coaching method, simply ask a question or two at most, and then return to the "normal" way of interacting. Do not make the strategy too obvious or revealing the first few times. Over the course of a number of conversations, introduce inquiry more frequently, gently coaxing the coachee to think more intensively for themselves. If the coachee calls out or labels what the coach is trying to do, the best strategy is to explain what is being done, to describe why the method is being used, and to name what could be gained by the coachee. This response might sound like:

✓ *My ideas may not be the best ones in this situation, and I would like to hear some of yours in addition to my own. Then together perhaps we can both decide what is the best strategy to take.*

✓ *I have realized that I jump in too quickly with people and am too directive. I would like to step back and give you some space to think this through.*

Or if push comes to shove:

✓ *You are correct; I am trying something new with you. I am asking you questions to get you to think about some options. If I continue to always tell you my ideas, I am stunting your growth as a leader and a professional. I see tremendous possibilities for you, and I want to help you to advance in your career.*

✓ *I have been working on honing my coaching skills. This is a method where I, as coach, provide you space to explore your situation and come up with your own possibilities and solutions. It may seem awkward, I know, but I believe it could be a useful process for both of us. My intention is to help you enhance your leadership skills. Would it be helpful going forward if I told you when I wanted to try some coaching with you?*

A second common challenge to coaching is that the leader has trouble finding the time to invest in coaching. This is a real issue, as days are filled with meetings, engagements, reports, emails, phone calls and interruptions. Coaching takes conscious effort, but it does not often have to be a huge investment in time to have a marked return on investment. It can take the form of simply one or two questions. It works because the leader maintains the habitual mindset to develop other leaders.

In *The Power of Habit*, Charles Duhigg describes how mindset drives behaviors through a simple and often mindless pattern of cue, routine, and reward.[26] A leader can change his or her habits by noticing these unconscious patterns and developing new ones. Engaging in this process, the leader can create a habit to develop other leaders – changing the mindless pattern of giving advice into a conscious choice of stealth coaching. Ironically, by developing the habit to coach, coachee's improve in self-sufficiency and the leader finds he or she has reclaimed more time.

Another strategy is to schedule a coaching session on the calendar. If an employee interrupts at an inopportune time with a situation that is coachable, schedule a meeting in the near future to discuss it. This can be handled simply, by stating:

✓ *This sounds intriguing. I do not have time at this moment to discuss it, as I have this report to complete. Let's look at the calendar, and set up a time to talk at the earliest opportunity this afternoon. Will that work for you?*

Additionally, it is important to note that a coaching conversation does not have to go to completion in one interaction. It is vital to recognize that coaching can be an ongoing discussion. If approached when the moment does not allow for an in depth conversation, it is completely appropriate to leave the coachee with a good coaching question and an invitation to pick up the conversation later. For example:

✓ *I have to get to my next meeting. In the meantime, consider what might be causing this confusion between you and this person. What might be at the root of it? And if you could have the interaction again, what would you do differently? Think about that and let's pick it up when I get back from my meeting.*

✓ *You appear stuck. Given how you have handled similar issues in the past, what might you try this time? Think about that and we can talk more over lunch.*

✓ *If you were in my position, what would you say to you? Mull that over tonight. I have to get to my appointment, but I want to talk further. Please add a meeting to my calendar for tomorrow.*

A third common barrier to using coaching is the temptation to manage versus lead. When approached with a situation or issue, there are essentially two lenses through which to examine the moment (as noted in chapter 9, The Coaching Mindset). Looking at it as a manager, one sees a task to resolve, a procedure or policy to unfurl and share, or an issue to be fixed. The manager holds the hammer, and the employee's issue is the nail to pound down. As a leader, one looks upon the same situation and becomes a developer, seeing an opportunity to empower the employee. This change of perspective allows for flexibility in handling challenges and interruptions.

Some issues are clearly management issues. These occur when there is one clear way of handling the situation at hand, and the manager's job is to instruct (teach, inform, direct) the employee on what to do. A good manager may also educate the employee on why something needs to be done a certain way. Other issues are in the leadership domain. These occur when the situation does not require one clear solution, and the leader recognizes that his or her way may not be the best way. The leader may have a personal bias that his or her solution is the best, and yet the leader who chooses to coach understands that to lead means not to force one's own preferred methods.

> *In the moment, when the heat is on, how does the leader assess and choose which approach to take? A simple strategy*

is to make the conscious choice to always start any interaction
by asking at least one question.

This will make inquiry a habit for the coach and develop a culture where asking questions is a norm. By asking a few clarifying questions at the beginning of an encounter, the leader can assess if the situation calls for management or leadership actions. Have reminders, or cues, to ask questions at the start. Place a sticky note on the computer, wear a rubber band on the wrist, make interruptions a cue to take a long deep breath and get focused. Keep a cheat sheet on the desk loaded with good questions or perhaps just a single word: "QUESTIONS." Each human being learns uniquely, so finding the best reminders and cues is an individual process. Ask, "What helps me remember to brush my teeth or to turn off the lights before I leave the house in the morning or to make plans with friends or family?" Uncovering the basic signs in routines can help inform how to make new ones and to create good habits of inquiry.

Dog-Ear These Ideas

- ✓ *Focus on your habits to change your interaction style. Aggressively seek to ask questions first, rather than jumping automatically into giving solutions.*

- ✓ *Understand that stealth coaching is a choice, and be prepared to share your strategy and intention when warranted.*

- ✓ *Remember the big picture: Coaching is an ongoing process of developing other leaders. Depending on time and complexity, sometimes coachees will be able to reach solutions and action plans in one conversation. Other times it may take a number of conversations.*

- ✓ *Your calendar is your friend. If there is not enough time to dive into coaching at the moment, schedule a time in the near future. And leave the coachee with at least one question to ponder before you reconvene to discuss the topic further.*

Yeah, But...

There are many reasons not to use stealth coaching. And there are just as many reasons to do so. Here are some of the most common resistors and solutions to engaging with the material in this book:

1. *Yeah, but... Doesn't this stuff take a lot of time?*

   The most common excuse people use to not try stealth coaching is that it appears to take too much time. Most people do not have fifteen minutes here and twenty minutes there to drop everything during the course of a work day and give their full focus and attention to a coachee. Stealth coaching conversations do not have to end with completely realized results, that is, ones that take the coachee all the way through to a fully developed plan of action.

   In fact, often stealth coaching occurs in "small bites," one or two short questions that plant seeds for the coachee to contemplate. Additionally, a stealthful coaching conversation may occur over a number of interactions. The coach always leaves the coachee with something to consider until they next have a chance to pick up the conversation.

   And, think of time commitment this way: Leaders spend plenty of time in directive or unproductive conversations with employees. Coaching may not take more time; it may just replace the time spent less productively using old management patterns.

2. *Yeah, but... What if they need an answer immediately?*

The leader gets to make a determination in every interaction with coworkers: Is this a coaching opportunity? If the building is on fire, smoke is pouring into the hallway, and your coachee runs into your office announcing the emergency, it is most likely not the time to start a line of inquiry with your coachee, "Interesting. Given the nature of what you describe, what do you see as your options?" Not every conversation is a coaching conversation. And, it is vital for the leader not to be easily influenced by a coachee if/when he or she describes a situation with pressing exuberance. Nor is it advisable to let the coach's pressing schedule or stress effect the use of coaching techniques. Take a moment to determine: Is this really an "emergency" where time is of the essence? Am I impatient right now due to my own deadlines? Be sure of what is truly going on before simply defaulting to solution giving. People love giving their monkeys away, especially when they know the leader is so adept at taking them.

3. *Yeah, but... When do I know when to coach or to just give my solutions?*

Use this three-phase process to recognize coaching situations versus solution-giving situations:

A. Is this issue something that can only be resolved one way? For example, is there a relevant standard operating procedure, policy, rule, or process that would settle the issue? If so, this is a situation best resolved by the management techniques of explaining, directing, or educating.

B. Are there multiple ways in which this issue could be resolved? Does the situation invite problem solving, decision making, or a complexity of thought beyond one solution? If so, this is a coaching situation best addressed by listening, asking questions, and moving the coachee towards discovering his or her own possible solutions and action steps.

C.   Are you moving too fast, multitasking, or in some other way being distracted and not able to give the proper time and attention to clearly assess the situation? If so, slow down before deciding on your approach with the coworker. Choosing the wrong strategy can result in more work for you, more dependency by your team, and a stagnant, under-performing organization. Choosing the right strategy can provide huge benefits to the coachee's professional growth, your success as a leader, and a high performing, motivated, and inspired organization.

4.   *Yeah but... Aren't there times when it is best to give my opinion or input?*

Yes. Sometimes giving your opinion is the best approach. Even in these cases, it is important to remember that giving direct advice can also serve as a spring board to return to coaching. For example, when James meets with Kate to plan for the conversation she will have with his boss, Pam, Kate explains what she wants to say to Pam, including "I want to start off by telling her how important this program will be to our organization and the difference it will make to our customers." Supposing James has worked with Pam for many years and knows, through experience, that Pam likes to hear the budget and bottom line first, before anything else. Once Pam sees how it will work financially, then she is open to hearing about impact and implementation.

For James to withhold this information from Kate is ludicrous, as he know she is destined to fail with her current plan of action. James can provide this important advice and yet return to coaching. He can tell Kate, "I have worked with Pam for almost fifteen years, and I know that if you start this meeting by telling her the big picture, she will shut down and become resistant. She wants to know how it will work financially first, before getting into anything else. So given that, how might you open the conversation now?"

James' advice to Kate is sound, and it will support her success with Pam. However, he still has not told Kate exactly what to do. Rather, he immediately returned to challenge her to figure out her next steps with Pam. This is a successful method for introducing information or providing feedback in the midst of a coaching conversation.

5. *Yeah, but… I can't always rely on others to get things done right, if through coaching they come up with their own solutions.*

Embedded in this statement are assumptions and perceptions that can undercut one's stealth coaching initiative. This kind of statement portrays a belief that only the leader has the ideal resolution to the situation. However, it is likely that in 99.9% of all work place situations, other people have done the same or similar work in the past, and other people will do the same or similar work in the future. To stake claim of being the only expert at a piece of work is presumptuous. This attitude carries implications that, "No one can deliver the level of quality I can on this," or that "There is not enough time to show someone else how to do this," or that "It is my rear end on the line, so I had better do it myself." Saying you can't rely on the ideas a coachee brings to the situation means that you do not in fact trust the coachee.

Leaders who trust their followers and build respectful rapport with them foster a highly motivated and creative workforce. In today's work environment, failure to delegate or to give others the opportunity to adopt new challenges, to make mistakes, and to thereby learn and to grow constitutes a failure of leadership. Though there are certainly times that a leader may not provide opportunities to others (time constraints, office politics, or resource challenges), there is a difference between actual constraints and the leader's choice to use his or her narrative as a way maintain control.

6.   *Yeah, but... Look, this stuff is just too "touchy feely" for me.*

This is possibly the most common rebuttal to using stealth coaching. Some find the coaching style of interaction to be way out of their comfort zones. In this case of discomfort, leaders can: do what they've always done and get what they've always gotten (i.e. doing others' work for them and creating relationships of dependency). Or, they can realize that employees do not develop their capacities automatically and that leaders themselves must change their styles of fostering growth in their employees. There are many strategies to develop the talent and capabilities of others, and coaching is proven to be one of the strongest leader tools available.

It may be helpful, especially early on when first getting used to this new mentality and methodology, to focus on the science of stealth coaching. The process of improving one's listening skills is the ideal place to start. When the impulse to provide an answer or make a suggestion enters the leader's mind, use it as a catalyst to listen more attentively and to remain quiet past one's typical comfort zone. The science of good stealth coaching, the science of exemplary leadership, begins with attentive listening. It is the greatest and most efficient tool for building rapport, trust, and respect, the key foundational components for effective stealth coaching. Another systematic strategy is to create a cheat sheet for oneself, listing quality questions and reminder cues. Keep the cheat sheet out and available as a handy reminder to utilize the stealth coaching process.

7.   *Yeah, but… This stuff doesn't seem rigorous enough.*

Engaging others as a stealth coach is, for many, a very different experience from what they are used to. Many people have workplace success because of their abilities to solve problems and get things done, and stealth coaching turns those problem solving notions on their head. Stealth coaching is not answer giving, directing, or taking on others' problems. Because of this, stealth coaching may at first appear too passive, too different from their typical style of interacting. Habits are powerful tools, especially when they have provided success in the past. However, author and executive coach Marshall Goldsmith states as his book, What Got You Here Won't Get You There:[27] The further one moves up in an organization, the less job success is about technical proficiency and the more it is about people ability.

Coaching involves is a new type of rigor for many leaders, and the new skill set for coaching is just as critical to business success as is any technical knowledge. A talented leader is expected to leverage other people to accomplish the organization's goals. As compared to command and control methods of management, coaching involves different competencies and different standards of leadership performance. Coaching competence demands rigorous application of new modes of inquiry, listening, support, and employee development. Be rigorous! Get out of your own way, get rid of your old mindset, and become a catalyst who helps others become great leaders themselves.

8.   *Yeah, but… How do I know if a person is ready or willing to be coached?*

The best way to find out the coachee's readiness for coaching is to do one of two things: (1) Try it out by asking a few questions and notice the coachee's responsiveness; or (2) Ask the coachee if he or she is open to discussing the situation further. If in the first option the coachee responds favorably to being asked questions, move further into the coaching process. If the coachee does not respond in a receptive way, stop coaching and ask the person how you can help them with the situation at hand. In the second option, if the coachee is open to discussing the topic, begin asking a few clarifying questions to see if they will move deeper into coaching. If the coachee resists the coaching, be transparent. Let the person know you would like to coach them through the situation, but if that is not preferable to him or her, ask how you can be of useful support.

9.   *Yeah, but... How can I coach someone who doesn't want to be coached?*

Sometimes coaching doesn't work. For a person to be receptive to coaching, there must be at least some level of trust, respect, and rapport between the coach and coachee. Before trying to coach someone, the leader should assess these aspects of their relationship. If any of these indicators are low, they need to be improved before attempting to coach.

Additionally, resistance may not be a result of the relationship between the coach and coachee. Rather, a timing or topic issue may be fueling the coachee's resistance. For example, someone may be excited, open, and receptive to being coached when it is a topic he or she likes. However, if the topic is something with which he or she is uncomfortable, it will be more challenging to coach through that issue. Timing is also important to consider. The leader may have a very high-performing employee who is typically open to being coached, but on a particular day or after a particular event, the employee may not be in a good "head space" or mindset to be open to coaching.

In each of these scenarios, it does not mean coaching cannot be a useful tool. It simply means it is not the right tool *right now*. Consider what needs to be in place for the coachee to be open to being coached: trust, topic, and timing. See chapter 13 (First Steps) for additional ideas on this topic.

10. *Yeah, but… What if someone resists my attempts at stealth coaching?*

It is inevitable that at times some people will resist the leader's attempt to coach. Though stealth coaching is a viable strategy, it is important to remember that people are by nature resistant to change, especially when change means not getting the usual results – in this case, quick answers, ideas, or solutions.

Do not be deterred by resistance! Early on, it may be appropriate to introduce stealth coaching in small bites before defaulting to old habits of providing answers and solutions. Start by asking only one or a few questions. Continue introducing stealth coaching gradually, "training" others over time in how this interaction works and what is expected of them.

11. *Yeah, but... What if the person I need to coach just shuts down or goes silent?*

It is not uncommon for a coachee to take long pauses of silence, especially when the coach asks a powerful question (one which gets the coachee to be reflective or self-referred). Be patient when these moments occur in coaching conversations. However, if the silence is a result of resistance or rejection of the coaching, it may be an indicator to try a different strategy. Stealth coaching can be effective, even if it needs to be eventually revealed as a strategy. In some instances it can be helpful to both the relationship and the coaching conversation to label what is happening. See chapter 20 (Overcoming Predictable Barriers and Challenges) for additional ideas.

12. *Yeah, but... What if I'm not very good at coaching? Can I do harm?*

It is highly unlikely a leader can cause undue harm to another by trying out the skills of stealth coaching. In the worst-case scenario, coachees call the leader on his or her attempts to coach them and the leader can then become more candid about the coaching strategy. Alternately, if the coachee becomes defensive or resentful, the leader can then resort back to other more traditional leadership strategies.

13. *Yeah, but... What if the person I need to coach doesn't trust me (we have bad history, we just don't get along, I cannot stand him or her, etc.)?*

Read #10 above and then ask yourself:

Is it worth it to you (or necessary) to have a productive relationship with this person? It is tough to be an effective leader while keeping people at arm's length. However, if the relationship is broken beyond repair, there are far bigger problems to deal with than simply wishing you could coach that person. There is also a difference between a challenging relationship and laziness, frustration, or resistance to conflict on the part of the coach or coachee. Explore all these dynamics before making a decision about how to proceed.

14. *Yeah, but... How do I stealth coach my challenging boss?*

There is no magic bullet to improve a bad boss. Given that, there is tremendous possibility to coach one's boss, if a few basic components are in place prior to coaching. First, does the boss see you as a high performer? If not, it is likely he or she would not be influenced by you in the first place, as you are not seen as providing value to them. Second, what is the level of trust and openness between you and the boss? The higher these factors are, the more likely the boss would be open to coaching.

First, figure out what metrics your boss uses to assess high performance in an employee. Are these measures ones you are willing and able to meet? You may need to adjust your effort, work style, or values to be seen as high performing. If so, are you willing to take these steps? For some, these changes are manageable, and for others the changes may be too dramatic or may violate personal values. The important thing to recognize is that, in either case, you are the one to decide whether you want to make certain personal changes to be seen by your superior as a high performer.

Second, if trust and openness need to be nurtured between you and the boss, how might that rapport grow? Do you need time with or access to this person? Do you need to break down your own resistance to building this relationship? If the boss seems unapproachable, what can you learn from someone who has a decent level of rapport with this person? If you want to build trust with someone you may find hard to approach, are you willing to work through your unease in service of the greater good? If you think you can work through these questions and considerations to build trust with a challenging boss, you may very well succeed in coaching that person. If the barriers are too daunting, then stealth coaching is simply not your tool for this situation.

A Note on Patience

The coach needs to bear in mind that not all results are immediately obvious. People need time to change behavior. What appears like a "no brainer" to one person may involve intensive awareness and effort to another, and vice versa. Patience is a key value of stealth coaching. Some coachee and organizational changes and results will certainly be immediately evident, and others will not. In reviewing the list of success indicators in chapter 6 (What Are Noticeable Results of Stealth Coaching?), one can determine which results may be seen in the short term, over moderate periods, and with longer investments of time and energy.

Coaching is not about instant gratification. Individual and organizational payoffs arise over the time, as coaching becomes part of organizational culture.

Additionally, becoming a competent, confident stealth coach does not happen overnight. No one is perfect. When attempts do not go well, forgive yourself and try again.

A competent stealth coach partners with other stealth coaches to help each other learn through mutual experiences and with mutual respect. Even good coaches need coaching.

As John Quincy Adams, 6th President of the United States said:

> *"If your actions inspire others to dream more, learn more, do more and become more, you are a leader."*

… And, perhaps as well, a fantastic stealth coach.

CLOSING

Afterward: A Note from the Author

Thank you for taking time to look over this book. I hope you have found value in it. I would love to hear about your successes, your failures, your challenges, questions, and concerns. Please feel free to contact me at: StealthCoachingBook@gmail.com. I will personally respond to your message.

Good luck on your leadership journey!

Sincerely,

Rob Kramer

References

[1] Olivero, Gerald K., Denise Bane, and Richard E. Kopelman. (1997). Executive coaching as a transfer of training tool: Effects on productivity in a public agency. *Public Personnel Management* 26:461.

[2] Phillips, J.J. and P.P. Phillips. (2007). Show me the article: The use of ROI in performance improvement. *Performance Improvement* 46(9):8-22.

[3] Oncken, Willima Jr. and Donald L. Wass. (1974). Who's got the monkey. *Harvard Business Review*, November-December.

[4] Joyce, Bruce. (1987). Paper presented at the Staff Development Awareness Conference, Columbia, South Carolina, January.

[5] Menges, Robert J. (1987). Colleagues as catalysts for change in teaching. *To Improve the Academy* 6:83-93.

[6] Menges, Robert J. (1987). Colleagues as catalysts for change in teaching. *To Improve the Academy* 6:91.

[7] International Coach Federation. (2009). *ICF global coaching client study.* Retrieved from http://www.coachfederation.org/includes/media/docs/ExecutiveSummary.pdf.

8 Muskingum College Cognitive Processes Classes. (1997). "History of Cognitive Psychology," Accessed March 19, 2012. http://www.muskingum.edu/~psych/psycweb/history/cognitiv.htm.

9 Cambell, M., Baltes, J.I, Martin, A., & Medings, K. (2007). The stress of leadership. Retrieved from http://www.ccl.org/leadership/pdf/research/StressofLeadership.pdf.

10 Gallup. (1998). Employee engagement: What's your engagement ratio? Retrieved from http://www.gallup.com/consulting/121535/employee-engagement-overview-brochure.aspx.

11 Pink, D. (2009). *Drive: The surprising truth about what motivates us*. New York, NY: Riverhead Trade Publishing.

12 Pink, D. (2010, January 27). "Drive: The surprising truth about what motivates us." [Presentation]. *The RSA*. Retrieved from http://www.thersa.org/events/audio-and-past-events/2010/drive-the-surprising-truth-about-what-motivates-us.

13 IBID

14 Kouzes, J. M. & Posner, B.Z. (2008). *The leadership challenge* (4th ed.). New York, NY: Jossey-Bass.

15 De Saint Exupery, A. (1942). *Flight to arras*. New York, NY: Harcourt, Brace & Company.

[16] McGregor, D. (2006). *The human side of enterprise.* New York, NY: McGraw-Hill.

[17] Zander, B. & Zander, R.S. (2002). *The art of possibility: Transforming professional and personal life.* New York, NY: Penguin Group.

[18] Gallup Business Journal. (2012). Item 12: Opportunities to learn and grow. *Gallup Business Journal.* Retrieved from http://businessjournal.gallup.com.

[19] Partnership for Public Service. (2012). Overall index scores for employee satisfaction and commitment. Retrieved from http://bestplacestowork.org/BPTW/rankings/overall/large.

[20] Cable News Network. (2012). 100 Best companies to work for. Retrieved from http://money.cnn.com/magazines/fortune/best-companies/2012/snapshots/1.html.

[21] Covey, S. (2004). *Seven habits of highly effective people.* New York, NY: Free Press.

[22] Allen, M.B. (1995). *Listening: The forgotten skill.* San Francisco, CA: Wiley, John & Sons.

[23] Csikszentmihalyi, M. (2008). *Flow: The psychology of optimal experience.* New York, NY: Harper Perennial.

[24] Redmon, R.E. (2000). Inquiry as the driver of coaching. *Coaching Skills for Federal Executives*, 17-20.

[25] Wurman, R.S. (2000). *Information anxiety 2* (2nd ed.). Indianapolis, IN: Que.

[26] Duhigg, C. (2012). *The power of habit.* New York, NY: Random House.

[27] Goldsmith, M. (2007). *What got you here won't get you there.* New York, NY: Hyperion.

About the Author

Rob Kramer provides leadership coaching and consulting for government, higher education, private and Fortune 500 companies, non-profits, and health care organizations. He has consulted with organizations in the U.S., Europe, Central and South America, and Africa. His coaching clients include CEOs, public and private sector executives, political appointees, managers, and entrepreneurs. Rob has worked fifteen years in management, including as Training & Development director at the University of North Carolina, where he provided coaching, consulting, and leadership development for 12,000 faculty and staff. He founded the Center for Leadership & Organizational Excellence at NC A&T State University, and was executive director for two non-profits. Rob is president of Kramer Leadership, LCC, a firm dedicated to maximizing the talent of mission-driven leaders and teams, and is adjunct faculty at the Federal Executive Institute. Rob recently lectured at TEDx, speaking on The Opposite of Stress. The presentation can be viewed at: www.KramerLeadership.com.

CPSIA information can be obtained
at www.ICGtesting.com
Printed in the USA
FFOW03n0933281117
43798096-42731FF